Marked copy

HENRY JAMES AND
ROBERT LOUIS STEVENSON

HENRY JAMES
AND
ROBERT LOUIS STEVENSON

A RECORD OF FRIENDSHIP
AND CRITICISM

Edited with an Introduction by
JANET ADAM SMITH

RUPERT HART-DAVIS : LONDON
1948

Published in association with The Classic Art Company

PRINTED IN GREAT BRITAIN BY RICHARD CLAY AND COMPANY, LTD.,
BUNGAY, SUFFOLK

CONTENTS

Number		Page
	Introduction by Janet Adam Smith	9
	Note on the text	49
1	*The Art of Fiction*, by Henry James, 1884	53
2	*A Humble Remonstrance*, by Robert Louis Stevenson, 1884	86
3	James to Stevenson, Dec. 5th, 1884	101
4	Stevenson to James, Dec. 8th, 1884	102
5	Stevenson to James, Oct. 28th, 1885	105
6	*Henry James*, a poem by Robert Louis Stevenson, 1885	108
7	The Stevensons to James, Feb. 25th, 1886	109
8	Stevenson to James, March 7th, 1886	112
9	Stevenson to James, July 29th, 1886	116
10	Stevenson to James, Jan. 1887	116
11	Stevenson to James, Feb. 1887	118
12	Stevenson to James, Aug. 22nd, 1887	121
13	Stevenson to James, Sept. 1887	122
14	*Robert Louis Stevenson*, by Henry James, 1887	123
15	Stevenson to James, Oct. 1887	160
16	James to Stevenson, Oct. 30th, 1887	163
17	Stevenson to James, Nov. 1887	165
18	James to Stevenson, Dec. 5th, 1887	167
19	Stevenson to James, March, 1888	169
20	Stevenson to James, May 28th, 1888	172
21	James to Stevenson, July 31st, 1888	173
22	Stevenson to James, March, 1889	177

CONTENTS

Number		Page
23	James to Stevenson, April 29th, 1889	180
24	Stevenson to James, Feb. 19th, 1890	182
25	James to Stevenson, March 21st, 1890	183
26	James to Stevenson, April 28th, 1890	186
27	Stevenson to James, Aug. 1890	190
28	Stevenson to James, Dec. 29th, 1890	192
29	James to Stevenson, Jan. 12th, 1891	196
30	James to Stevenson, Feb. 18th, 1891	203
31	Stevenson to James, Oct. 1891	206
32	Stevenson to James, Dec. 7th, 1891	208
33	James to Stevenson, March 19th, 1892	211
34	James to Stevenson, April 15th, 1892	214
35	Stevenson to James, Dec. 5th, 1892	217
36	James to Stevenson, Feb. 17th, 1893	220
37	Stevenson to James, May 19th, 1893	223
38	Stevenson to James, June 17th, 1893	223
39	James to Stevenson, Summer, 1893	228
40	Stevenson to James, July, 1893	232
41	James to Stevenson, Aug. 5th, 1893	233
42	James to Stevenson, Oct. 21st, 1893	238
43	Stevenson to James, Dec. 1893	241
44	Stevenson to James, July 7th, 1894	242
45	Stevenson to James, Nov. 24th, 1894	246
46	James to Fanny Stevenson, Dec. 1894	247
47	*The Letters of Robert Louis Stevenson*, by Henry James, 1899	250
	Index of Books, Stories and Authors	281

ILLUSTRATIONS

Henry James, by John S. Sargent, 1886
Facing page 81
Robert Louis Stevenson, by John S. Sargent, 1885
Facing page 96
Facsimile of letter from the Stevensons to James
Pages 109–10
Facsimile of poem by Stevenson *Pages* 113–14
Facsimile of letter from Stevenson to James *Page* 121
Facsimile of fragment of letter from James to Stevenson
Pages 229–30

INTRODUCTION

CRITICS AND READERS rarely couple the names of Henry James and Robert Louis Stevenson. In the houses where James's novels are a long row in the study, most of the Stevensons are up in the nursery or schoolroom, beside *The Three Midshipmen* and *The Coral Island*; in those where Stevenson is the chief literary ornament, in the uniform dignity of the Swanston Edition, or the Skerryvore, or the Tusitala, there is likely to be no book by James at all. Yet in their lifetime the two men were linked, not only by the closest ties of personal affection, but by a common concern for the craft of the novelist, and for the whole art of literature, that was shared by very few English-speaking writers of their day.

James and Stevenson first met at Bournemouth, in the spring or early summer of 1885; Stevenson was thirty-four, and the publication of *Treasure Island* had recently added a general popularity to the *succès d'estime* which he had won with *An Inland Voyage*, *Travels with a Donkey*, and various short stories and essays. James, at forty-two, was known as the author of *Roderick Hudson*, *The American*, *The Portrait of a Lady*, *Daisy Miller*, and a number of critical articles. Stevenson, who had spent the last four years at Davos and Hyères, had gone to Bournemouth on account of his health; James had brought his invalid sister there for a few weeks. During the next two years there were frequent meetings—long evenings at Skerryvore, the Stevensons' house on the West Cliff, and at Sidney Colvin's house in the British Museum, where the Stevensons stayed on their visits to London. But in 1887 the Stevensons sailed for America; the following years took them to San Francisco, the Marquesas, Hawaii, Tahiti, Sydney, and finally Samoa, but never back to Europe. Henry James, who had seen them off at Tilbury with a case of champagne for the voyage, followed their doings 'with an aching wing, an inadequate geography and an ineradicable hope'; and the friendship made in Bournemouth flourished in the letters that sped between London and the South Seas till Stevenson's death in 1894.

In this friendship there are several themes. Of the personal liking and affection between the two men the letters that follow speak plainly enough. There is an equal warmth in the reference that each made to the other when writing or talking to a third person.* 'James writes the kindest, most affectionate letters,' wrote Stevenson to Colvin in 1888, 'I have a warm heart to that man.' When the news of Stevenson's death reached London, James went at once to their mutual friend Mrs. Sitwell, crying,

* William James certainly knew of his brother Henry's feeling. Once, when chidden by a Harvard colleague in a Boston street-car for buying the English edition of *Prince Otto* instead of the pirated American one, his answer was, 'Well, ordinarily when buying books I don't mind stealing, but I thought I wouldn't steal from Stevenson.'

'It isn't *true*, it isn't *true*, say it isn't true.' And to Edmund Gosse he wrote:

'Of what can one think, or utter or dream, save of this ghastly extinction of the beloved R.L.S.? It is too miserable for cold words—it's an absolute desolation. It makes me cold and sick—and with the absolute, almost alarmed sense, of the visible material quenching of an indispensable light. That he's silent forever will be a fact hard, for a long time, to live with. To-day, at any rate, it's a cruel, wringing emotion. One feels how one cared for him—what a place he took; and as if suddenly *into* that place there had descended a great avalanche of ice. I'm not sure that it's not for *him* a great and happy fate; but for us the loss of charm, of suspense, of "fun" is unutterable.'

Even five years later, writing again to Gosse, he owned that 'I find myself, somehow, unable to think of Louis in these days (much more to speak of him) without an emotion akin to tears.'

Stevenson inspired affection in a great number of people, but none of his friends brought to the relationship quite the insight and sympathy of Henry James. In one way it was an easier relation for James than it became for Henley, or Colvin, or Louis's cousin Bob Stevenson. As he had never known Louis in his bachelor days, James had no strong possessive feelings, and did not start with a prejudice that Louis alone was a far better friend than Louis married. Colvin, indeed, was soon on good terms with Fanny Stevenson (though his first reaction on meeting her in 1880 had been to doubt whether he could ever 'get reconciled to the little determined brown face and white teeth and . . . grizzling hair, which we are to see beside him in future'); but to the others she was too often the intruder, whose constant care of Louis's health they interpreted as a wish to keep him from them. James, however, got on extremely well with her from the first. 'We are devoted to him, and he comes to us every evening after dinner,' she wrote to Colvin from Bournemouth: 'He seems very gentle and comfortable.' 'He is gentle, amiable, and soothing,' she described him to her mother-in-law (also noting that 'he looks like the Prince of Wales'). When James dined with them, the only guest, on their wedding anniversary, Fanny Stevenson prepared special American dishes in his honour, and he responded by taking two helpings of everything.

Henley, with his loud, boisterous talk and sanguine plans for making a fortune by writing plays, quite exhausted her husband, and her discouragement of his visits was a main cause of his quarrel with Stevenson. The visits from friends and relations, anxious to see Louis after his years abroad, imposed a constant strain on his health and his wife's temper during the Bournemouth days. But there was never any complaint about James. 'We have had a good deal of wearing company for some time,' confided Fanny Stevenson to Colvin in 1885:

'Our own house was full, and we had also a couple of dependencies in the neighbourhood. Louis's mother and father were here. Aunt Alan, and Miss Ferrier and Henley, we have also had Teddy Henley for a couple of nights. Bob and his family, and Katharine and hers are also in the neighbourhood,—and Sam's here. It has been such a difficult party that I quite broke down under the strain.

'Through it all the dear Henry James remained faithful, though he suffered bitterly and openly. He is gone now, and there is none to take his place. After ten weeks of Henry James the evenings seem very empty, though the room is always full of people.'

We have James's own report, in a letter also addressed to Colvin, of a visit later in the year:

'My visit had the gilt taken off by the somewhat ponderous presence of the parents—who sit on him much too long at once. (They are to remain apparently another week, and I can't see why *they* don't see how they take it out of him). He was bright and charming, but struck me as of a smaller vitality than when I saw him last—a very frail and delicate thread of strength. If he could be quite alone on alternate, or occasional, weeks, it would be a blessing.'

Some of Fanny Stevenson's long letters to James have survived, and they throw a little light on the Bournemouth evenings of 1885. She speaks of the days 'when you sat enthroned in your own blue chair, and we grouped ourselves about you, and quaffed the different flowing bowls, and held sweet converse.' It is tempting to suppose that the conversation between the two men turned often on the drama. Stevenson had recently been working with Henley on *Beau Austin*, *Admiral Guinea*, and the English version of *Macaire*; and James's life-long interest in the theatre had lately expressed itself in critical articles and in the dramatisation of *Daisy Miller*, while the possibilities of *The Tragic Muse* (which he began to write two years later) were already glimmering before him.* William Archer, the dramatic critic, was another new-made friend of Stevenson and frequent visitor at Skerryvore. But the probability is that talk of the drama did not go very far. Fanny Stevenson, for one, would have been likely to discourage it: she had had quite enough of Henley rushing down with a bagful of plans for plays and a determination to knock off one or two at high speed with Louis. 'Henley must not come to him now with either work or business unless he wishes to kill him,' she had written to Mrs. Sitwell, and nine years later Stevenson remembered how he had stuck to the writing of *Admiral Guinea* through 'the waves of faintness and nausea' that followed a hæmorrhage.

In any case, there was a great disparity in the two men's interests. Henry James was a regular playgoer, while Stevenson had not been inside a theatre since his return from America in 1880, and had never been as susceptible as James to the glamour of stage life.† He never seems to have taken himself seriously as a dramatist, and was angry with Henley for hawking round *Macaire* ('a piece of job-work, hurriedly bockled') and *Admiral Guinea*,

* *The Notebooks of Henry James*, edited by F. O. Matthiessen and Kenneth B. Murdock (1947): entry for June 19th, 1884.
† See James's Preface to *The Tragic Muse*.

which he described to his collaborator as 'a low, black, dirty, blackguard, ragged piece: vomitable in many parts—simply vomitable.' Whereas Stevenson was probably honest in saying that his main interest in the theatre was money ('The theatre is the gold-mine,' he had written to his father in 1883, 'and on that I must keep an eye'), James's protestations that *his* plays were only written out of financial necessity seem to mask his deeper desire to reach a wider public than that which read his novels. Such at least was the opinion of his nephew Henry James.* And the apologetic note of some of his later references to the theatre in letters to Stevenson may be due to his awareness of the disparity of their interest.†

To conversation about the novel, though, each could contribute an equal zest. As will be shown more fully later in this introduction, James and Stevenson had an awareness of the mysteries and possibilities of their craft that was shared by hardly any other English novelist. And talk of their own work raised no discords in the Skerryvore circle, as talk of Stevenson's plays did. Fanny Stevenson, no less than Louis, was a warm admirer of James's stories—she thought his power of creating children wonderful, and the boy in *The Author of Beltraffio* reminded her of a child of her own who had died ten

---

* Leon Edel: *Henry James: Les Années Dramatiques* (1931), p. 92.
† It was *before* meeting Stevenson, and knowing only of their joint work through Henley, that James had written to Mary Anderson the actress that 'they are both full of ideas, especially dramatic ideas, and of knowledge of the stage' (Leon Edel: *op. cit.*, p. 241).

years before. But the tone of all the Bournemouth letters —Stevenson's, James's, and Fanny Stevenson's—shows how closely James entered into *all* the family interests and preoccupations, from Louis's relations with his doctor to difficulties with the proofs of *Prince Otto*. And it was not only Fanny and Louis that he charmed. He had been critical of the way the old Stevensons tired Louis out on their visits: but when Thomas Stevenson was dying (so reported Fanny) he said after a silence, 'I wonder how that dear man is now?'—and it was Henry James he meant.

When Stevenson had transformed himself from an invalid in Bournemouth into a traveller, adventurer, and unofficial chieftain in the South Seas, James was still the friend who most sympathetically projected himself into the new life. Other friends at home were grieved by Stevenson's absence, hurt at his decision to spend the rest of his life away from them, jealous of activities that lay beyond their own scope, and critical of any work done, or appreciation received, in places and circumstances remote from their own experience. When the American publisher S. S. McClure visited London in 1888 he was surprised by the note of detraction in the talk of Stevenson's friends:

'Some of his friends there, those in whose critical powers he had most faith, were always condemning his new book, whatever it was. They could stand for what was already printed, but when he sent them the manuscript of a new work, they usually declared that that was fatal, that would be the end, and entreated him, for the sake of his reputation, not to publish it. . . . He was not judged with the same leniency as other writers of his time. These criticisms of his friends were often the highest expressions of their solicitude and regard; they were often very helpful to Stevenson, but sometimes disheartening.'

But 'there was one most marked exception to this dissenting chorus,' McClure noted,

'and that exception was Henry James, to whom Stevenson had given me a letter. I had somehow always imagined Mr. James as a rather cold and unsympathetic man, but I now found how greatly I had been mistaken. His tone about Stevenson warmed my heart. His warm human friendship was a delight after what I had been hearing. There was nothing at all critical in his attitude. He was Stevenson's friend, admirer and well-wisher. His interest in Stevenson's health, his work, his plans for the future, was wholly affectionate, wholly disinterested. His loyal, generous feeling I have never forgotten. He questioned me minutely about everything pertaining to Stevenson. His interest was keen, sympathetic, personal.'

Stevenson's decision finally to settle in Samoa hurt and puzzled his London friends still further. Colvin openly admitted that

'I persuaded myself that from living permanently in that outlandish world and far from cultivated society both he and his writing must deteriorate. . . . Translating unconsciously my own need and desire for his company into a persuasion that mine was needed, as of old, for criticism and suggestion to him in his work, and that he no longer valued it, I wrote reproachfully, pleading against and prophesying evil from his purpose.'

Andrew Lang, after reading some letters from Stevenson, decided that 'the Samoan politics, like all politics, are a bore'; and Colvin complained that the monthly budget of news from Vailima contained too much about local affairs, and too many natives. 'Please remember,' answered Stevenson, 'that my life passes among my "blacks or chocolates." If I were to do as you propose, in a bit of a tiff, it would cut you off entirely from my life. You must try to exercise a trifle of imagination, and put yourself, perhaps with an effort, into some sort of sympathy with these people, or how am I to write to you? I think you are truly a little too Cockney with me.' Gosse was even more Cockney: 'the fact seems to be,' he wrote to G. A. Armour after reading *The South Seas*, 'that it is very nice to *live* in Samoa, but not healthy to *write* there. Within a three-mile radius of Charing Cross is the literary atmosphere, I suspect.'

From this parochialism Henry James was entirely free. He never made the mistake of confusing literature with London literary gossip, and could tell Stevenson that 'the mere thought of you is better company than almost any that is tangible to me here, and London is more peopled to me by your living in Samoa than by the residence of almost anybody else in Kensington or Chelsea.' James, who didn't like adventurous holidays, could enter sympathetically into every detail of the South Sea life, and took every opportunity to keep himself informed. When Stevenson's mother and his stepson Lloyd Osbourne came home on visits, James sought them out and plied them with questions; he was always eager to step round to the British Museum to get the latest news of Vailima from Colvin; and Graham Balfour, Stevenson's cousin and biographer, reported after a visit to London that James could take a First in any Samoan subject.

James indeed shared Colvin's regret that they should miss Stevenson so much more than he appeared to miss them, and he was grateful for any sign 'that he hasn't forgotten a fellow—or sacrificed one wholly to cannibal friendships.' He too found the island personalities and politics 'almost squalid,' and he could not but regret the claims made on Stevenson's energy by these Samoan affairs, his work on his own estate, and his hospitality to missionaries, natives, and British sailors. James loved Stevenson's prose, and grudged all effort that went elsewhere, even into verse. When Stevenson was busy on his own house, the 'sense of his clearing the very ground to be able to do his daily work' was agony to James. But, as he wrote to Colvin, commenting on 'Louis's wondrous lustiness,'

'In the face of such facts how can one grudge his really *living*—with such an apparent plenitude of physical life, no matter how literature suffers? Oh, yes, I'm afraid it *must* suffer, it can't help it. But we must change our point of view, and be thankful for what survives, what he can still give us. After all he has *bien du talent*!'

James never forgot what the alternative would be; that the life of often distracting action was simply the price Stevenson was paying for having any life at all. Where Gosse and the others spoke as if Stevenson might have been, should have been, leading a literary life within the three-mile radius, James understood Stevenson when, in answer to inquiries if he didn't regret his exile, he begged his friend to 'remember the pallid brute that lived in Skerryvore like a weevil in a biscuit.'

Beyond James's personal affection for Stevenson there lay his interest in Stevenson's whole situation. The man living under the daily threat of a fatal hæmorrhage, yet with such an appetite for the active life; the novelist who could only gain the health and energy for writing at the risk of dissipating them on other ends; the writer who had to spur his talent to earn more and more money to pay for the life of action that kept him alive; the continual tug between the claims of life and literature—here was a situation not unlike those which had provided James with the germ of a novel or story. Something of this feeling is evident in a letter to William James in 1887, where Henry speaks of Stevenson as 'a most moribund but fascinating being, of whom I am very fond. If he were in health he would have too much "side" as they say here, but his existence hangs but by a thread, and his almost squalid invalidism tones down the " 'Ercles' vein" in him, as well as any irritation one may feel from it. He has a most gallant spirit and an exquisite literary talent.' This aspect of the relationship is again stressed in the essay on Stevenson's Letters in which James speaks of this man 'launched into the world for a fighter with the organism of, say, a composer,' and writes so tenderly of the last heroic struggle to reconcile the art of the novelist with the practical duties of the large householder:

'It all hung, the situation, by that beautiful golden thread, the swinging of which in the wind, as he spins it in alternate doubt and elation, we watch with much of the suspense and pity with which we sit at the serious drama. It is serious in the extreme; yet the forcing of production, in the case of a faculty so beautiful and delicate, affects us almost as the straining of a nerve or the distortion of a limb.'

Beyond Stevenson's individual situation, moreover, there was the whole Stevenson circle to entertain and fascinate James.* Like D. H. Lawrence thirty years later,

* This circle was not, however, in James's mind when he wrote *The Author of Beltraffio*, as has often been supposed—for instance, by George S. Hellman in his article in the *Century Magazine*, January, 1926, on *Stevenson and Henry James: The Rare Friendship between Two Famous Stylists*. Mr. Hellman builds a considerable edifice on the assumption that James knew all about the alleged destruction by Mrs. Stevenson, at Hyères, of a novel Stevenson wrote about a street-walker, and used the incident as the germ of

Stevenson had the capacity to arouse interest and controversy wherever he went. During the years that James knew him he moved, again like Lawrence, in a cloud of friends, family and hangers-on. There was always his wife, and almost always his step-son Lloyd Osbourne; we have seen the crowd which clustered round him at Bournemouth; when he sailed to America his mother came too, and a French maid; his step-daughter Isobel Strong came to live with them at Vailima with her boy. James appreciated the whole troupe: 'They are a romantic lot—and I delight in them,' he wrote when they sailed for America; and even after Louis himself had gone he talked of them as 'those people—who are very touching and interesting to me,' and 'these poor women—infinitely touching and interesting.' He was alive to Fanny Stevenson's limitations: 'Poor lady, poor barbarous and merely *instinctive* lady,' he once characterised her; and 'Only remember,' he warned Gaillard Lapsley, who thought of visiting her in California, 'that *she* (with all deference to her) was never the person to have seen, it was R. L. S. himself.' Yet he grasped that, for all her shortcomings, for all the burdens that her family laid on Stevenson's shoulders, she was possibly the only person who could have kept Stevenson alive to write at all.

---

his story (which was published before the writers had met). But an entry in James's *Notebooks* for March 26th, 1884 shows that the *donnée* of *The Author of Beltraffio* came to him from an anecdote about John Addington Symonds.

INTRODUCTION

After Stevenson's death, James found a painful interest in observing what the others did with him—how they made him a public figure, how they exploited their association, how they made a flourishing business out of him, how they fell out with each other over his memory. Fanny Stevenson and Lloyd Osbourne had their tiffs with Colvin; all three joined in a common irritation at the waywardness of Charles Baxter, Stevenson's old Edinburgh crony and man of business. Many of these cross-currents were apparent in the affair of Stevenson's biography, in which James played an unwilling part. Colvin had been going to write it: but Lloyd Osbourne and Fanny Stevenson (whose feeling about her husband was such that she thought Samoa should be made a British protectorate because his body was buried there) considered that Colvin was being hopelessly dilatory and unsympathetic, and entrusted the work to Graham Balfour instead. When Lloyd Osbourne was in London in 1899 negotiating the change, he tried to enlist James's help, and showed him the whole correspondence on the matter. James, on returning the letters, confined himself to expressing interest in the 'dramatic and human' correspondence, and satisfaction that the matter was settled; then a day or two later was horrified to learn that Colvin had been given a somewhat misleading impression of his remarks. 'I had no wish whatever,' he hastily assured Colvin, '—but every wish, of the intensest character, the other way, to be approached by Lloyd on the question of any matter connected with the Life.' The situation was clearly interesting, the falling-out of friends, the contrast between the over-enthusiastic family (who had their own practical reasons for wishing to establish Stevenson as a sound literary security) and the over-cautious friends. Again, it was a theme for a James *nouvelle*; but James shied away immediately from the prospect of being personally involved in it. With just such alacrity he had already avoided one embroilment, when he learnt that Stevenson had nominated him one of his executors. 'I immediately wired,' he reported to Colvin, 'a profoundly regretful, but unconditional and insurmountable refusal'; and we may guess that his refusal was dictated as much by his reluctance to be involved in a delicate personal situation as by his inexperience in business matters. As late as 1907, hearing that Fanny Stevenson might be coming to England, he was divided between a wish to see her and a wish not to be embroiled once more.

James and Stevenson clearly loved each other; but they also needed each other. 'The Polonius and the Osric of novelists' may have been Thomas Hardy's tart view; but they certainly were the two most conscious novelists of their time in England. They thought more profoundly about their art, and cared more intensely for it, than any of their contemporaries—Hardy, Meredith, Kipling. They had both read widely among the great French novelists; they had a background of European literature; there is never a sign of provinciality in their criticism. The 1884 articles in *Longman's* with which this record opens showed each how much the other shared this seriousness: and Stevenson's first letter to James is a model for literary controversy: 'I want the whole thing well ventilated, for my own education and the public's, and I beg you to look as quick as you can, to follow me up with every circumstance of defeat where we differ, and (to prevent the flouting of the laity) to emphasise the points where we agree.' To 'establish a thoughtful interest in the art of literature' was the all-important question; neither was concerned with scoring points in argument. Stevenson had already realised that any artist working with a deliberate purpose ran the risk of finding no fit audience; but from this minute he knew that he had one reader who would always understand what he was doing.* He had no doubt which of them was the better artist: 'I seem to myself a very rude, left-handed countryman; not fit to be read, far less complimented, by a man so accomplished, so adroit, so craftsmanlike as you.' What mattered was that they should both recognise that novel-writing was an exacting art; and their criticism of each other's work in their

* There was another man who read him with as much insight and understanding as James, but Stevenson never knew of it. Gerard Manley Hopkins, who had already enjoyed *The New Arabian Nights*, in 1883 read *A Gossip on Romance* and the short story *The Treasure of Franchard*, and wrote of them in a letter to R. W. Dixon that shows his awareness and appreciation of Stevenson's intentions (*The Correspondence of Gerard Manley Hopkins and Richard Watson Dixon*, 1935, pp. 114–15; see also *Letters of Gerard Manley Hopkins to Robert Bridges*, 1935, pp. 228, 236–9, 251).

letters was acute and technical, one craftsman speaking to another. They discussed the key and tone of a novel; the lighting of an incident; the point of view; the difficulties of realising the original conception.

A few of James's early stories, notably *Daisy Miller*, had been widely read and admired. But there is little evidence that his London friends had any very warm appreciation of his full-length novels, or any intelligent understanding of his aims and workmanship. To W. D. Howells, after the publication of *The Bostonians* and *The Princess Casamassima*, he wrote sadly, 'They have reduced the desire, and the demand, for my productions to zero'. Stevenson's first poem from Bournemouth shows his immense enjoyment of the early stories, but the enjoyment did not stop short with *Daisy Miller*. His workman-like comments on *Roderick Hudson* and *The Princess*, mingling appreciation of the aim with criticism of detail—'May I beg you . . . to go over the sheets of the last few chapters, and strike out "immense" and "tremendous"? You have simply dropped them there like your pocket-handkerchief'—obviously gave James enormous pleasure. Possibly he was even more heartened by Stevenson's immense gusto for all his work—except *The Portrait of a Lady*. Stevenson reading *Roderick Hudson* to his wife and mother round the fire at Saranac; searching the bookshops of Sydney for a copy of *The Tragic Muse*; writing delighted doggerel at Vailima about Adela Chart—these must have offered some compensation for a public almost totally indifferent and for literary friends polite but dense. Sending *The Tragic Muse* out to Samoa, James wrote that 'seriously and selfishly speaking, I can't (spiritually) afford *not* to put the book under the eye of the sole and single Anglo-Saxon capable of perceiving—though he may care for little else in it—how well it is written.'

This dependence on each other is all the more striking in that James and Stevenson numbered among their friends the best literary company of the time. Yet James was exasperated by Meredith, who had nothing more to say of a novel than that he 'liked it' or 'didn't like it so much'; while Stevenson found that even Colvin could be dense and remark that there was 'an artistic problem of a kind' in *The Ebb-Tide*—as if there could ever *not* be one! The quotation from McClure has shown how Stevenson's friends were apt to carp and nag, to wish him to repeat past successes instead of breaking new ground. Henley and Colvin would judge a new work by the standards of a past success and find it faulty, not realising that Stevenson was off on an entirely different line. Henley took *The Merry Men* as another story of adventure, and thought it unconvincing: Stevenson had to make it clear to him that its real hero was the sea.

As for the public in general, Stevenson, whose work sold well, had as low an opinion of it as James, who hardly sold at all ('I *don't* sell ten copies! ... But I never mention it—nearer home'). In a letter to Gosse in 1886 Stevenson wrote:

'What the public likes is work (of any kind) a little loosely executed; so long as it is a little wordy, a little slack, a little dim and knotless, the dear public likes it; it should (if possible) be a little dull into the bargain. I know that good work sometimes hits; but, with my hand on my heart, I think it is by an accident. And I know also that good work must succeed at last; but that is not the doing of the public; they are only shamed into silence or affectation.... There must be something wrong in me, or I would not be popular.'

Later it was 'that great, hulking, bullering whale, the public'; and a year before his death Stevenson warned a younger writer that 'the little, artificial popularity of style in England tends, I think, to die out; the British pig returns to his true love, the love of the styleless, of the shapeless, of the slapdash and the disorderly.' 'One must go one's way,' declared James to his brother William, 'and know what one's about and have a general plan and a private religion—in short, have made up one's mind as to *ce qui en est* with a public the draggling after which simply leads one in the gutter.'

They were constantly vigilant, even with each other, to discriminate between writing and journalism, art and manufacture. 'He is all smart journalism and cleverness: it is all bright and shallow and limpid, like a business paper—a good one, *s'entend*,' were Stevenson's second thoughts on Kipling, to whose work James had introduced him; he was careful to emphasise that his own history of Samoa was only 'journalism,' his own *Wrecker* 'a machine' (though James found it 'a brave and beautiful' one). When he reported his amusement in novels by Anstey and Marion Crawford, James protested, 'I can't go with you three yards in your toleration. . . . I make no bones to proclaim them shameless *industriels* and their works only glories of Birmingham.'

They both felt the degradation of public taste, the disesteem of art, the carelessness of writers towards their craft, as a national disgrace: to them it was the artist's duty, as much as the soldier's, to keep his country's credit high. 'I look on, I admire, I rejoice for myself,' wrote Stevenson on receiving *Soldiers Three*, 'but in a kind of ambition we all have for our tongue and literature I am wounded. If I had this man's fertility and courage, it seems to me I could heave a pyramid.' 'If it hadn't been for *Catriona*,' wrote James in 1893, 'we couldn't, this year, have held up our head. It had been long, before that, since any decent sentence was turned in English.' And, pleading with Colvin for an early publication of *Weir of Hermiston* ('the thing he was so splendidly doing when he died'), James spoke of it as a matter 'that touches so the very essence of Louis's *honour*.' This pride can be matched in only one contemporary, Gerard Manley Hopkins, to whom 'a great work by an Englishman is like a great battle won by England.'

What each of the two delighted to recognise in the other was a sense of the height and sacredness of art—and its appalling demands. Stevenson's criticism of Scott was based on Scott's apparent obliviousness of these demands. It grieved him that 'a man of the finest creative instinct' should be so often utterly careless of style and construction; and he felt that Scott had lost as well as gained because 'of the pleasures of his art he tasted fully; but of its toils and vigils and distresses never man knew less.'* There was never any word between James and Stevenson of quickly and easily dashing off a book; it was always talk of re-writing, re-drafting, beginning again, altering in proof, a snail's rate of progress. 'That is the hard part of literature. You aim high, and you take longer over your work, and it will not be so successful as if you had aimed low and rushed it.' But when the demands seemed too much, Stevenson had that 'glimmer of faith (or hope) which one learns at this trade, that somehow and some time, by perpetual staring and glowering and rewriting, order will emerge'; and James could believe in 'all the high sane forces of the sacred time fighting, through it, on my side!' About work produced in that temper there could be no question of self-conceit, of personal pride; James and Stevenson delighted freely in their own creations, but always with the loving detachment of the genuine artist towards something now complete in itself, and so no longer part of him—never with the embarrassed modesty or mock modesty of the imper-

* 'While I was at the Reays' I took up one of Scott's novels—*Redgauntlet*; it was years since I had read one. They have always a charm for me—but I was amazed at the badness of *R*.: *l'enfance de l'art.*' (*The Notebooks of Henry James*, entry for Dec. 26th 1881.)

fect artist who cannot separate the thing he has made from his own personality. James fondling Mrs. Gereth or Hugh Vereker, Stevenson hugging Thrawn Janet or David Balfour, are proud as artists, conscious of the privilege of working at such intensity, never for one instant self-complacent.

'O the height and depth of novelty and worth in any art! and O that I am privileged to swim and shoulder through such oceans! Could one get out of sight of land—all in the blue! Alas not, being anchored here in flesh, and the bonds of logic being still about us.

 'But what a great space and a great air there is in these small shallows where alone we venture! and how new each sight, squall, calm, or sunrise!'

This confession of Stevenson, made to Henley when he was thirty-two and 'merely beginning to commence to prepare to make a first start at trying to understand my profession,' can be set without incongruity beside the testament, written only for himself, that was discovered among James's papers after his death:

'I come back, I come back, as I say, I all throbbingly and yearningly and passionately, oh mon bon, come back to this way that is clearly the only one in which I can do anything now, and that will open out to me more and more, and that has overwhelming reasons pleading all beautifully in its breast. What really happens is that the closer I get to the problem of the application of it in any particular case, the more I get *into* that application, so that the more doubts and torments fall away from me, the more I know where I am, the more everything spreads and shines and draws me on and I'm justified of my logic and my passion.'

James and Stevenson were both strong in opposing the growing realism of the novel, recognising that a work of imagination must live by its own laws and only take so much from life as serves its purpose. Neither had any use for the raw, untrimmed 'slice of life'. Once, after an afternoon's talk with a new acquaintance, Stevenson wrote 'I feel as if I could put him in a novel with effect; and ten to one, if I know more of him, the image will be only blurred.' James, hearing in a neighbour's casual remark at a dinner-party the germ that was to grow into *The Spoils of Poynton*, endured agony in having to listen to 'the fatal futility of fact' that the end of the tale revealed. 'Man's one method,' wrote Stevenson, 'whether he reasons or creates, is to half-shut his eyes against the dazzle and confusion of reality.... The novel, which is a work of art, exists, not by its resemblances to life, which are forced and material, as a shoe must still consist of leather, but by its immeasurable difference from life, which is designed and significant, and is both the method and the meaning of the work.'

Another point of similarity was that Stevenson (who has so often been held up as an example of manly cheerfulness and optimism) and James each had an abnormally acute sense of evil. Zola and other realists mirrored the tangible, visible, smellable evil of lust, poverty, squalor.

To James and Stevenson these material horrors were but manifestations of a darker power inherent in the order of things; and to convey this power was the work of the deepest imagination, not of the camera-eye.

With both men, awareness of evil was closely bound up with early circumstances and inheritance. James experienced it through three members of his family—his father, his sister, and his brother William. At the time when the future novelist was only a year old, his father had been staying with the family near Windsor, apparently in good health and cheerful spirits, when he suddenly suffered what he called a 'vastation' which reduced him 'from a state of firm, vigorous, joyful manhood to one of almost helpless infancy.'

'To all appearances it was a perfectly insane and abject terror, without ostensible cause, and only to be accounted for, to my perplexed imagination, by some damnèd shape squatting invisible to me within the precincts of the room, and raying out from his fetid personality influences fatal to life.'

Later, he wrote a volume on *The Nature of Evil*. William James described a similar experience of his own, 'when suddenly there fell upon me without any warning, just as if it came out of the darkness, a horrible fear of my own existence.' 'Physical pain, however great, ends in itself and falls away,' wrote Alice James the day before she died, 'whilst moral discords and nervous horrors sear the soul.'

Stevenson, too, could observe in his father the stresses and strain caused by a constant awareness of evil. Old Thomas Stevenson was a man, his son tells us, of 'a profound essential melancholy of disposition,' filled with 'a morbid sense of his own unworthiness.' Stevenson's early letters to Mrs. Sitwell describe a man of strongest passions and fiercest conscience, whose storms and scenes, when they disagreed on religion, politics, or Louis's future, would reduce the son to spiritual misery and physical collapse. Stevenson speaks of his father on his knees, wrestling in prayer, and of 'a whole world of repressed bitterness under the calm of daily life.' There is black horror behind Stevenson's anguished cry, 'He has told me that he is a weak man, and that I am driving him too far.' No doubt Thomas Stevenson's sense of evil, like his son's, owed much to the Scottish Presbyterian tradition, which made men conscious of the evil stalking through the world beside them. But with most Scots this consciousness took a more homely and personal form: the Devil is a familiar enough figure in Scottish folklore and literature, and is as likely to be referred to (as in Burns) by half-affectionate as by awful terms. But Thomas Stevenson's dark horrors comprised more than the figure of Auld Clootie.

Neither Henry James nor Louis Stevenson seems to have been subject to just such visitations as their fathers were: yet there is no question that they were abnormally aware of the presence of evil. Lying in bed as a child on stormy nights Stevenson shuddered at 'the evil spirit that was abroad.' His cry to Mrs. Sitwell, 'In bed at night I often make up my mind that tomorrow I shall begin to descend to the mouth of the pit,' may have its element of melodrama: but it shows that hell and damnation were concepts firmly fixed in his mind. Colvin, who thought of Stevenson as 'a focus of cheerfulness,' once came unexpectedly on him in the garden at Skerryvore and 'he turned round upon me a face such as I never saw on him save that once—a face of utter despondency, nay tragedy, upon which seemed stamped for one concentrated moment the expression of all he had ever had, or might yet have, in life to suffer or to renounce.' Henry James, on emerging from a period of illness, wrote to Elizabeth Robins that 'I was wholly unfit to be alone, and in terror of being so. Then followed a black bad time (of horrible nervous illness and melancholia) over which I drop the veil.' As Professor Matthiessen has noted, 'in a more enduring way than either his father or his brother had done, he kept throughout life the sense of the abyss always lurking beneath the fragile surface.'

Evil to both, then, was a prime reality of the world, which could not be excluded from their art. But there could be no question of presenting it by direct realistic methods—even if we stretch these words to include direct realistic descriptions of ghosts and demons.* Evil could

---

* It is interesting to compare these two authors' presentation of evil with that of some of their contemporaries. In Wilkie Collins

never be as limited or defined for James or Stevenson: they were too well aware of the bad things that lie inside each human soul, of the evil inherent in the universe that cannot be explained or exorcised by the unmasking of a spook or demon. James posed the artistic problem that this conception raised in discussing *The Turn of the Screw*.

'Portentous evil—how was I to save that, as an intention on the part of my demon-spirits, from the drop, the comparative vulgarity, inevitably attending, throughout the whole range of possible brief illustration, the offered example, the imputed vice, the cited act, the limited deplorable presentable instance? ... One had seen, in fiction, some grand form of wrong-doing, or better still of wrong being, imputed, seen it promised and announced as by the hot breath of the Pit—and then, all lamentably, shrink to the compass of some particular brutality, some particular immorality, some particular infamy portrayed: with the result, alas, of the demonstration's falling sadly short.'

Later, discussing the particular case of the corruption of the children by the governess and valet, he concluded that

'There is for such a case no eligible *absolute* of the

---

the bad things are felt as bogies that lurk, haunt, and may jump out at any moment. In the ghost stories of M. R. James the sense of horror is finally explained by some simple wrong act in the past, and is exorcised when the ghost or apparition is exposed or laid. In Arthur Machen the unimaginable horrors that the reader is promised narrow down to the survival of a horrible rite, or some other physical degradation. With Hardy evil is usually the random action of arbitrary supernatural powers. Among the writers who successfully conveyed the sense of moral evil might be mentioned Melville, Conrad, and Meade Falkner in *The Lost Stradivarius*.

wrong; it remains relative to fifty other elements, a matter of appreciation, speculation, imagination—these things moreover quite exactly in the light of the spectator's, the critic's, the reader's experience. Only make the reader's general vision of evil intense enough, I said to myself—and that already is a charming job—and his own experience, his own imagination, his own sympathy (with the children) and horror (of their false friends) will supply him quite sufficiently with all the particulars. Make him *think* the evil, make him think it for himself, and you are released from weak specifications.'

'Only make the reader's general vision intense enough'— this clearly was Stevenson's aim also, in such stories as *Thrawn Janet* or *Olalla*, and more particularly in *Jekyll and Hyde*. True, some of Hyde's evil actions are specified, but his murder of Sir Danvers Carew is felt to be no climax, not *the* evil action towards which he had been tending, but simply as one manifestation of a nature wholly bad. Again, there is nothing final about the first incident recorded, when Hyde collides with a little girl at a street crossing and 'trampled calmly over the child's body and left her screaming on the ground.' It is simply Stevenson using his favourite method of representing a situation, or an atmosphere, by one clear-cut dramatic picture. In this dreadful scene ('It sounds nothing to hear, but it was hellish to see. It wasn't like a man; it was like some damned Juggernaut') is implied the depth of Hyde's depravity—a man capable of that would be capable of anything.

Yet though neither writer weakened his case by over-particularising evil, it does not follow that he relied on vague impressions. Both James and Stevenson present the scene most vividly—the hushed quiet house and garden of *The Turn of the Screw*, the oppressive sultry weather of *Thrawn Janet*. In *Markheim* and *The Jolly Corner* there is as much sense of suspense, the footsteps in the empty house make our flesh creep just as effectively, as in the contrivances of the professional hair-raisers. To both writers the duality of man's nature was such a vital truth that it could, on occasion, only be adequately expressed in a real second person—in Jekyll's Hyde,* in the figure hiding his face at the foot of the stairs in *The Jolly Corner*. A further similarity may be found in the two writers' technical presentation. James, in *The Turn of the Screw*, and Stevenson, in *Jekyll* and *Thrawn Janet*, did not tell the story directly, but through one of the characters.

---

* The method of the Jekyll–Hyde change was widely criticised. James considered 'the business of the powders ... too explicit and explanatory' (see p. 157), and Robert Bridges complained to Gerard Manley Hopkins of the 'gross absurdity' of the means employed 'which is physical and should have been magical'. In his reply (*Letters to Bridges*, p. 238) Hopkins contended that 'it is not more impossible than fairies, giants, heathen gods, and lots of things that literature teems with'. Stevenson himself recorded (in his *Chapter on Dreams*, in *Across the Plains*) that 'the business of the powders, which so many have censured, is, I am relieved to say, not mine at all but the Brownies'—*i.e.* the creatures who spun tales for him while he slept. Possibly the development of the use of drugs in psychiatry has made us more ready than Stevenson's contemporaries to accept the plausibility of the change by chemical means.

The advantages of the method are that this character appears to the reader on the same plane of reality as the story; so that if the author has the ability to make the narrator convincing (like the young governess of *The Turn of the Screw*, with her vicarage background), he persuades the reader of the actuality of the horrors, and saves himself the much more difficult business of convincing him directly. Stevenson set *Thrawn Janet* so firmly into the mouth of an old man of Balweary that he ended by scaring himself with the tale.

These similarities in mood and outlook between James and Stevenson were accompanied by a considerable divergence of aims and methods. In their sympathy there was nothing of the mutual admiration of a persecuted coterie; and each could recognise the integrity of the other's work though it was not of his own kind. 'Stick to your own system of evocation so long as what you positively achieve is so big.' There are the obvious differences of subject-matter: in the one, flights in the heather, quests for buried treasure, the adventures of the gipsy, the rover, the bohemian: in the other, the great country-houses of England, the palazzos of Venice, the cultured and decadent Europeans, the refined and moneyed Americans. But more fundamental are the two different ways of seeing the given subject. When Stevenson thought of a new idea, he saw it at once in terms of chapter-headings, titles, names of characters; in his account of the genesis of *The Master of Ballantrae* he described how one incident occurred to him, then another, how the nature of the incidents determined what kind of characters the story should have. Sometimes he would reverse the process—take a character and choose incidents to develop it (as *Weir of Hermiston* began with his interest in Lord Braxfield); or his starting-point might be a place, like the Hawes Inn at Queensferry, from which *Kidnapped* was launched, or the cruel wreck-strewn coast of *The Merry Men*, and he would create actions and persons to express it. James saw a subject first as a *value*—something central, which every incident, character and scene should illuminate. Stevenson wrote *Treasure Island* to fit a map drawn for a boy's entertainment. When James described *The Awkward Age* to his publishers, he drew on a sheet of paper 'the neat figure of a circle consisting of a number of small rounds disposed at equal distance about a central object. The central object was my situation, my subject in itself, to which the thing would owe its title, and the small rounds represented so many distinct lamps, as I liked to call them, the function of each of which would be to light with all due intensity one of its aspects.' When we think of a James novel we have read long ago, what shines out from the mist of forgotten detail is this 'central object'—the generosity of Milly Theale, played on by the greed of others; the receptive innocence of Maisie; the beautiful richness of life in Paris as Lambert Strether saw it. But when we recall a Stevenson, it is Alan Breck and Cluny at cards in the Cage on Ben Alder; or the Master and Henry

Durie fighting in the frosty wood by candlelight; or the young man handing round the cream tarts in the oyster bar off Leicester Square. It is always a scene, as clearly outlined as the twopence-coloured scenes Stevenson had bought as a child for his toy theatre. It was, of course, a deliberately planned effect: 'Vital—that's what I am at, first, wholly vital, with a buoyancy of life. Then lyrical, if it may be, and picturesque, always with an epic value of scenes, so that the figures remain in the mind's eye for ever'. Stevenson did not lack interest in character, or the play of one personality on another; and James quoted the quarrel scene in *Kidnapped* as an example of the 'rare transparency' possible to the novel—'it can illustrate human affairs in cases so delicate and complicated that any other vehicle would be clumsy.' But with Stevenson it is only in terms of the scene that we can recapture the 'human affair.'

Then, again, the creative imagination worked very differently in the two authors. With James it was mainly a conscious process. He watched life for that little flicker that gives the turn of a story, and then built the story round it. With truly passionate intensity he scanned his situations, that none of their possibilities should escape him; yet his midnight appeals, confided to his Notebooks, strike one as directed rather to some tutelary deity, for strength to sustain his genius through the act of creation, than to his unconscious imagination. But Stevenson looked to the Brownies for scenes, incidents, even for whole plots. They gave him Hyde at the window; Hyde turning back into Jekyll; the meetings on the stairs in *Olalla*. They provided the clear-cut detail, and his waking imagination had to fill in the gaps: the method of poetry rather than prose. 'Unconscious thought, there is the only method . . . the will is only to be brought in the field for study and again for revision.' Yet Stevenson's next sentence, 'The essential part of work is not an act, it is a state', is also true of James; and each writer, while faithful to his own genius, could understand and appreciate the method of the other.

While James would always work on a subject from the outside, Stevenson would immerse himself, and draw his readers in with him. It is not the immersion of a daydream, and we are not to assume that, because so many of his novels are told in the first person, Stevenson wished to identify himself with the adventurer-hero. The figure of the narrator is always brilliantly clear, seen from every side; and often the form of narration is used for a calculated effect, that the action may be reflected through the mirror of one particular mind. Stevenson threw himself into his novels because his novels showed the kind of life he would like—not so much in the literal sense that he would have liked to go treasure-hunting with Jim Hawkins or have taken to the hills with David Balfour, as in the general sense that life appeared to him, at its most vivid and romantic, as scene and incident—a ship putting out from harbour with a dear cargo; a horseman rattling with his whip on the green shutters of an inn at midnight. Those moments of his life which gave him the acutest pleasure read most like incidents in his novels—a ride through the lines of a native army in Samoa, past the pickets at the ford; a sight of the rebel king at night 'galloping up our road upon unknown errands'; hearing a woman sing, deep in the forest.

These different aims in their novels were rooted in different attitudes towards life. For James, the life of the artist was enough; his keenest experience was the play of his 'inexhaustible sensibility' and his greatest wish that when he saw a new 'value' hovering before him, his genius should not fail. But Stevenson wanted the life of action as well. 'I ought to have been able to build lighthouses and write *David Balfours** too,' he wrote within a year of his death, remembering the 'pyramids and monuments' set by his forebears round the coasts of Scotland. He had deliberately chosen the life of a writer, and he had strenuously refused to be turned into an engineer or an advocate; but from the beginning his writings had envisaged life as action. All his works—particularly the essays on abstract subjects—abound with images of action: life is expressed in terms of travellers arriving at inns, sailors making landfall, armies setting out to the sound of drums. His health did much to emphasise his passion for physical activity. Not to be ill, not to be on his back, was in itself a joy; and to be able, as he was in Samoa, to walk all day

* Title of *Catriona* as published serially in *Atalanta*.

through the bush, to be in the saddle for five hours on end, to be out in the heat overseeing the building of his house, to sail among islands, to be drenched through and catch no cold—this was extraordinary happiness, a compensation for the years of coughing and blood-spitting at Davos, Hyères and Bournemouth. Those years of 'slow dissolution' made a sudden death seem the only good one—'I wish to die in my boots'; and he chose to be remembered in his epitaph as the sailor and the hunter. But the fundamental reason is that, passionately as he valued the life of art, he had not James's faith in his vocation. He had worked his talent faithfully, but knew it was not the greatest. 'I think *David Balfour* a nice little book, and very artistic, and just the thing to occupy the leisure of a busy man; but for the top flower of a man's life it seems to me inadequate.' 'My skill deserts me, such as it is, or was. It was a very little dose of inspiration, and a pretty little trick of style, long lost, improved by the most heroic industry. . . . I cannot take myself seriously, as an artist; the limitations are so obvious.' '0.6 of me is artist; 0.4, adventurer. . . . And if it had not been for my small strength, I might have been a different man in all things.'

James never questioned Stevenson's talent in his own field, and he grudged every atom of energy that was put into other activities than writing; he even grudged the energy spent on ballads, 'because I love so your divine prose and want the comfort of it. Things are various because we do 'em. We mustn't do 'em because they're various.' Further, as James realised, the life of action must be paid for. In 1892 Stevenson earned nearly £4000, but the new house at Vailima, the huge hospitality, the horses and the black boys and the roads through the bush, ate up every penny. The spectacle, as revealed in the published letters, was agony to James; and when Colvin was helping with the publication of a volume of Stevenson's occasional articles (*Across the Plains*, 1892), James could but express pain 'at seeing a great man so emptied —so pursued to his innermost lair; the *sac* so *vide*, the mystery, the backshop, the personal, i.e. the intellectual loneliness of the artist so invaded as the hungry booksellers and newspapers insist more and more on its being. But one is face to face with a public that gobbles as well as bullies.'

James never sacrificed art to life; yet (and in the author of *The Ambassadors* it is not surprising) there is nothing priggish in his attitude towards Stevenson, only warm human sympathy for the writer with no unearned income, for the man for whom 'life became bigger . . . than the answering effort could meet,' and exultation that, for all these demands, Stevenson should never be careless, never be shoddy, that to the end he should be capable 'of new experiments and deeper notes,' that at his death he should be working, in *Weir of Hermiston*, more brilliantly and surely than ever before. And yet James knew that the life of action would have to be paid for at last. With uncanny precision he foretold Stevenson's fate in a letter written to Gosse in 1901 on the publication of Graham Balfour's *Life*:*

'I see now that a really curious thing has happened. . . . Insistent publicity, so to speak, has done its work (I only knew it was *doing* it, but G. B.'s book's a settler), and Louis, *qua* artist, is now, definitely, the victim thereof. That is, he has *superseded*, personally, his books, and this last replacement of himself so *en scène* (so largely by his own aid, too) has *killed* the literary baggage.'

Very effectively the Stevenson legend *did* kill the literary baggage. Stevenson's stories continued to be read with avidity and delight; but Stevenson the serious writer was eclipsed by Stevenson the picturesque character—the imaginative invalid child, the rebellious Edinburgh bohemian, the Tusitala of the last coloured South Sea years. Much has been spoken and written about Stevenson in the half-century since he died: relations, friends and

---

* G. K. Chesterton, reviewing the *Life* in the *Daily News* of October 18th, 1901, discussed the possibility of 'an artistic sketch' being written of Stevenson, as distinct from a formal biography, and continued: 'Into it, as into every work of art, the personality of the author is bound to creep. Mr. Henley might write an excellent study of Stevenson but it would only be of the Henleyish part of Stevenson, and it would show a distinct divergence from the finished portrait of the Colvinesque part of Stevenson which would be given by Professor Colvin. The best man of all to write a book like this would be a professional novelist. A subtle and brilliant novelist who was a friend of Stevenson is ready to our hand, but let us remember that the portrait would not be Stevenson, but a composite photograph of Stevenson and Mr. Henry James.'

acquaintances, from the old nurse to the casual visitor at Vailima, have contributed their memories, admirers and detractors have scrutinised every chapter of his life, societies have been founded to honour his memory and preserve his relics. But in all this activity there has been next to no serious criticism of his writings. James and Stevenson wrote to each other as equally concerned in the continuous and fascinating struggle with words and situations; but whereas the study of James's novels has steadily grown till it has now become, in America at any rate, a major academic industry, Mr. Percy Lubbock is almost the only critic to have given the same serious attention to a novel by Stevenson that he gives to one by James. Stevenson wrote *Treasure Island* for a boy, and would be the last to complain that boys enjoyed him. But Stevenson, as André Gide and Alain-Fournier recognised, was more than a boy's writer. This record of the relationship between the two writers shows the encouragement that James received from having one critical and appreciative reader among his equals; and it may help to place Stevenson among the most conscious, conscientious and interesting novelists who have written in English. A generation that has never been bothered by hero-worship may perhaps be led to read *The Beach of Falesá* and *Thrawn Janet* with the same attention as *The Author of Beltraffio* and *The Turn of the Screw*, and find in reading them the same delight as once did Henry James.

JANET ADAM SMITH.

NOTE ON THE TEXT

This compilation contains all the letters that passed between James and Stevenson that I have been able to trace. We know that there were some that have not survived: when Stevenson was in the South Seas, several miscarried between England and Samoa, including a 'long and masterly treatise on *The Tragic Muse.*' It seems likely too that a number of the letters that James wrote to Stevenson at Bournemouth were lost or destroyed when the Stevensons left England in 1887. Six of the letters that follow, whose originals are in the Houghton Library of Harvard University, have not hitherto been published: Nos. 7, 9, 12, 37, 39, 45. The five by Stevenson were probably excluded from the collected edition of his letters on the grounds of their slightness; but they have their place in a specialised record like the present, where even a trivial note helps to establish the key and tone of a relationship.

The text of James's letters follows that of Mr. Percy Lubbock's edition of *The Letters of Henry James* (1920), except for No. 39, which is printed from a facsimile, and No. 46, printed from a typescript, now in the James collection at Harvard. This beautiful letter of condolence to Fanny Stevenson may be new to many James enthusiasts; it was first printed in Nellie Van de Grift Sanchez's

Life of Mrs. R. L. Stevenson (1920), and quoted in full by Colvin in an article on the two writers that appeared simultaneously in *Scribner's Magazine* and the *Empire Review* (March 1924). The text of Stevenson's letters follows, in the main, that of the Vailima Edition (1924), though No. 28 contains ten lines that were printed in *Letters to His Family and Friends* (1899) and then, without comment, omitted from the Vailima Edition. Nos. 7, 9, 12, 37 and 45 are printed from facsimiles. The lines *Henry James* (No. 6) are printed as they first appeared in *Underwoods* (1887); those on 'What the glass says' (No. 8) are printed from a facsimile. James's *The Art of Fiction* and Stevenson's *A Humble Remonstrance* (Nos. 1 and 2) follow the text of their original publication in *Longman's Magazine* (September and December 1884); and James's two articles on Stevenson follow the text of their original publication in the *Century Magazine* (April 1888) and the *North American Review* (January 1900). A few obvious misprints have been corrected, and a uniform style adopted for all titles of books, stories, articles and plays, and for the letter headings.

Sooner or later, the student of Stevenson finds that his gratitude to Sidney Colvin for preserving and collecting Stevenson's letters is swallowed up in exasperation at his handling of them. Where it is possible to check from originals, Colvin is shown as indifferent to punctuation, to the position of a word, to the change of a phrase, to the omission of a whole passage (as in No. 28, mentioned above). No. 17 in this collection was reproduced in facsimile in Vol. II of *Letters to his Family and Friends*; close scrutiny has revealed twenty-three points where the printed text departed from the facsimile which faced it. For the present record, it was not feasible to trace the originals of Stevenson's letters to James (except for the five letters and the poem already mentioned), and check the text; but it is to be hoped that a later editor may rescue all Stevenson's letters from the inaccuracies with which they have been beset.

My grateful thanks are due to:

The Librarian of the Houghton Library, Harvard University; The Director of the Fitzwilliam Museum, Cambridge; the Robert Louis Stevenson Club, Edinburgh, and in particular Mr. W. Dods Hogg; and Mr. E. J. Beinecke of New York; for letting me consult manuscript letters or photostats in their possession;

Mr. Leon Edel, Mr. Percy Lubbock, Professor F. O. Matthiessen, Mr. Simon Nowell-Smith, and Mr. Allan Wade, for letting me draw upon their vast knowledge of James;

The James family, for permission to reproduce James's letters, and the Author's Society, for permission to reproduce Stevenson's;

The Sargent Executors for permission to reproduce the two portraits, and Mr. John Payne Whitney for permission to photograph the Stevenson portrait, which is now in his possession.   J. A. S.

I

THE ART OF FICTION*

BY HENRY JAMES

I SHOULD not have affixed so comprehensive a title to these few remarks, necessarily wanting in any completeness, upon a subject the full consideration of which would carry us far, did I not seem to discover a pretext for my temerity in the interesting pamphlet lately published under this name by Mr. Walter Besant. Mr. Besant's lecture at the Royal Institution—the original form of his pamphlet—appears to indicate that many persons are interested in the art of fiction and are not indifferent to such remarks as those who practise it may attempt to make about it. I am therefore anxious not to lose the benefit of this favourable association, and to edge in a few words under cover of the attention which Mr. Besant is sure to have excited. There is something very encouraging in his having put into form certain of his ideas on the mystery of story-telling.

It is a proof of life and curiosity—curiosity on the part of the brotherhood of novelists, as well as on the part of their readers. Only a short time ago it might have been supposed that the English novel was not what the French

* Published in *Longman's Magazine*, September 1884, and reprinted in *Partial Portraits* (1888).

call *discutable*. It had no air of having a theory, a conviction, a consciousness of itself behind it—of being the expression of an artistic faith, the result of choice and comparison. I do not say it was necessarily the worse for that; it would take much more courage than I possess to intimate that the form of the novel, as Dickens and Thackeray (for instance) saw it, had any taint of incompleteness. It was, however, *naïf* (if I may help myself out with another French word); and, evidently, if it is destined to suffer in any way for having lost its *naïveté*, it has now an idea of making sure of the corresponding advantages. During the period I have alluded to there was a comfortable, good-humoured feeling abroad that a novel is a novel, as a pudding is a pudding, and that this was the end of it. But within a year or two, for some reason or other, there have been signs of returning animation—the era of discussion would appear to have been to a certain extent opened. Art lives upon discussion, upon experiment, upon curiosity, upon variety of attempt, upon the exchange of views and the comparison of standpoints; and there is a presumption that those times when no one has anything particular to say about it, and has no reason to give for practice or preference, though they may be times of genius, are not times of development, are times, possibly even, a little, of dulness. The successful application of any art is a delightful spectacle, but the theory, too, is interesting; and though there is a great deal of the latter without the former, I suspect there has never been a genuine success that has not had a latent core of conviction. Discussion, suggestion, formulation, these things are fertilizing when they are frank and sincere. Mr. Besant has set an excellent example in saying what he thinks, for his part, about the way in which fiction should be written, as well as about the way in which it should be published; for his view of the 'art,' carried on into an appendix, covers that too. Other labourers in the same field will doubtless take up the argument, they will give it the light of their experience, and the effect will surely be to make our interest in the novel a little more what it had for some time threatened to fail to be—a serious, active, inquiring interest, under protection of which this delightful study may, in moments of confidence, venture to say a little more what it thinks of itself.

It must take itself seriously for the public to take it so. The old superstition about fiction being 'wicked' has doubtless died out in England; but the spirit of it lingers in a certain oblique regard directed toward any story which does not more or less admit that it is only a joke. Even the most jocular novel feels in some degree the weight of the proscription that was formerly directed against literary levity; the jocularity does not always succeed in passing for gravity. It is still expected, though perhaps people are ashamed to say it, that a production which is after all only a 'make believe' (for what else is a 'story'?) shall be in some degree apologetic—shall renounce the pretension of attempting really to compete with life. This, of course, any sensible wide-awake story declines to do, for it quickly perceives that the tolerance granted to it on such a condition is only an attempt to stifle it, disguised in the form of generosity. The old Evangelical hostility to the novel, which was as explicit as it was narrow, and which regarded it as little less favourable to our immortal part than a stage-play, was in reality far less insulting. The only reason for the existence of a novel is that it *does* compete with life. When it ceases to compete as the canvas of the painter competes, it will have arrived at a very strange pass. It is not expected of the picture that it will make itself humble in order to be forgiven; and the analogy between the art of the painter and the art of the novelist is, so far as I am able to see, complete. Their inspiration is the same, their process (allowing for the different quality of the vehicle) is the same, their success is the same. They may learn from each other, they may explain and sustain each other. Their cause is the same, and the honour of one is the honour of another. Peculiarities of manner, of execution, that correspond on either side, exist in each of them and contribute to their development. The Mahometans think a picture an unholy thing, but it is a long time since any Christian did, and it is therefore the more odd that in the Christian mind the traces (dissimulated though they may be) of a suspicion of the sister art should linger to this day. The only effectual way to lay it to rest is to emphasize the analogy to which I just alluded—to insist on the fact that as the picture is reality, so the novel is history. That is the only general description (which does it justice) that we may give the novel. But history also is allowed to compete with life, as I say; it is not, any more than painting, expected to apologize. The subject-matter of fiction is stored up likewise in documents and records, and if it will not give itself away, as they say in California, it must speak with assurance, with the tone of the historian. Certain accomplished novelists have a habit of giving themselves away which must often bring tears to the eyes of people who take their fiction seriously. I was lately struck, in reading over many pages of Anthony Trollope, with his want of discretion in this particular. In a digression, a parenthesis or an aside, he concedes to the reader that he and this trusting friend are only 'making believe.' He admits that the events he narrates have not really happened, and that he can give his narrative any turn the reader may like best. Such a betrayal of a sacred office seems to me, I confess, a terrible crime; it is what I mean by the attitude of apology, and it shocks me every whit as much in Trollope as it would have shocked me in Gibbon or Macaulay. It implies that the novelist is less occupied in looking for the truth than the historian, and in doing so it deprives him at a stroke of all his standing-room. To represent and illustrate the past, the actions of men, is the task of either writer, and the only difference that I can see is, in proportion as he succeeds, to the honour of the novelist, consisting as it does in his having more difficulty in collecting his evidence, which is so far from being purely literary. It seems to me to give him a great character, the fact that he has at once so much in common with the philosopher and the painter; this double analogy is a magnificent heritage.

It is of all this evidently that Mr. Besant is full when he insists upon the fact that fiction is one of the *fine* arts, deserving in its turn of all the honours and emoluments that have hitherto been reserved for the successful profession of music, poetry, painting, architecture. It is impossible to insist too much on so important a truth, and the place that Mr. Besant demands for the work of the novelist may be represented, a trifle less abstractly, by saying that he demands not only that it shall be reputed artistic, but that it shall be reputed very artistic indeed. It is excellent that he should have struck this note, for his doing so indicates that there was need of it, that his proposition may be to many people a novelty. One rubs one's eyes at the thought; but the rest of Mr. Besant's essay confirms the revelation. I suspect, in truth, that it would be possible to confirm it still further, and that one would not be far wrong in saying that in addition to the people to whom it has never occurred that a novel ought to be artistic, there are a great many others who, if this principle were urged upon them, would be filled with an indefinable mistrust. They would find it difficult to explain their repugnance, but it would operate strongly to put them on their guard. 'Art,' in our Protestant communities, where so many things have got so strangely twisted about, is supposed, in certain circles, to have some vaguely injurious effect upon those who make it an important consideration, who let it weigh in the balance. It is assumed to be opposed in some mysterious manner to morality, to amusement, to instruction. When it is embodied in the work of the painter (the sculptor is another affair!) you know what it is; it stands there before you, in the honesty of pink and green and a gilt frame; you can see the worst of it at a glance, and you can be on your guard. But when it is introduced into literature it becomes more insidious—there is danger of its hurting you before you know it. Literature should be either instructive or amusing, and there is in many minds an impression that these artistic preoccupations, the search for form, contribute to neither end, interfere indeed with both. They are too frivolous to be edifying, and too serious to be diverting; and they are, moreover, priggish and paradoxical and superfluous. That, I think, represents the manner in which the latent thought of many people who read novels as an exercise in skipping would explain itself if it were to become articulate. They would argue, of course, that a novel ought to be 'good,' but they would interpret this term in a fashion of their own, which, indeed, would vary considerably from one critic to another. One would say that being good means representing virtuous and aspiring characters, placed in prominent positions; another would say that it depends for a 'happy ending' on a distribution at the last of prizes, pensions, husbands, wives, babies, millions, appended paragraphs and cheerful remarks. Another still would say that it means being full of incident and movement, so that we shall wish to jump ahead, to see who was the mysterious stranger, and if the stolen will was ever found, and shall not be distracted from this pleasure by any tiresome analysis or 'description.' But they would all agree that the 'artistic' idea would spoil some of their fun. One would hold it accountable for all the description, another would see it revealed in the absence of sympathy. Its hostility to a happy ending would be evident, and it might even, in some cases, render any ending at all impossible. The 'ending' of a novel is, for many persons, like that of a good dinner, a course of dessert and ices, and the artist in fiction is regarded as a sort of meddlesome doctor who forbids agreeable aftertastes. It is therefore true that this conception of Mr. Besant's, of the novel as a superior form, encounters not only a negative but a positive indifference. It matters little that, as a work of art, it should really be as little or as much concerned to supply happy endings, sympathetic characters, and an objective tone, as if it were a work of mechanics; the association of ideas, however incongruous, might easily be too much for it if an eloquent voice were not sometimes raised to call attention to the fact that it is at once as free and as serious a branch of literature as any other.

Certainly, this might sometimes be doubted in presence

of the enormous number of works of fiction that appeal to the credulity of our generation, for it might easily seem that there could be no great substance in a commodity so quickly and easily produced. It must be admitted that good novels are somewhat compromised by bad ones, and that the field, at large, suffers discredit from overcrowding. I think, however, that this injury is only superficial, and that the superabundance of written fiction proves nothing against the principle itself. It has been vulgarised, like all other kinds of literature, like everything else, to-day, and it has proved more than some kinds accessible to vulgarisation. But there is as much difference as there ever was between a good novel and a bad one: the bad is swept, with all the daubed canvases and spoiled marble, into some unvisited limbo or infinite rubbish-yard, beneath the back-windows of the world, and the good subsists and emits its light and stimulates our desire for perfection. As I shall take the liberty of making but a single criticism of Mr. Besant, whose tone is so full of the love of his art, I may as well have done with it at once. He seems to me to mistake in attempting to say so definitely beforehand what sort of an affair the good novel will be. To indicate the danger of such an error as that has been the purpose of these few pages; to suggest that certain traditions on the subject, applied *a priori*, have already had much to answer for, and that the good health of an art which undertakes so immediately to reproduce life must demand that it be perfectly free. It lives upon exercise, and the very meaning of exercise is freedom. The only obligation to which in advance we may hold a novel without incurring the accusation of being arbitrary, is that it be interesting. That general responsibility rests upon it, but it is the only one I can think of. The ways in which it is at liberty to accomplish this result (of interesting us) strike me as innumerable and such as can only suffer from being marked out, or fenced in, by prescription. They are as various as the temperament of man, and they are successful in proportion as they reveal a particular mind, different from others. A novel is in its broadest definition a personal impression of life; that, to begin with, constitutes its value, which is greater or less according to the intensity of the impression. But there will be no intensity at all, and therefore no value, unless there is freedom to feel and say. The tracing of a line to be followed, of a tone to be taken, of a form to be filled out, is a limitation of that freedom and a suppression of the very thing that we are most curious about. The form, it seems to me, is to be appreciated after the fact; then the author's choice has been made, his standard has been indicated; then we can follow lines and directions and compare tones. Then, in a word, we can enjoy one of the most charming of pleasures, we can estimate quality, we can apply the test of execution. The execution belongs to the author alone; it is what is most personal to him, and we measure him by that. The advantage, the luxury, as well as the torment and responsibility of the novelist, is that there is no limit to what he may attempt as an executant—no limit to his possible experiments, efforts, discoveries, successes. Here it is especially that he works, step by step, like his brother of the brush, of whom we may always say that he has painted his picture in a manner best known to himself. His manner is his secret, not necessarily a deliberate one. He cannot disclose it, as a general thing, if he would; he would be at a loss to teach it to others. I say this with a due recollection of having insisted on the community of method of the artist who paints a picture and the artist who writes a novel. The painter *is* able to teach the rudiments of his practice, and it is possible, from the study of good work (granted the aptitude), both to learn how to paint and to learn how to write. Yet it remains true, without injury to the *rapprochement*, that the literary artist would be obliged to say to his pupil much more than the other, 'Ah, well, you must do it as you can!' It is a question of degree, a matter of delicacy. If there are exact sciences there are also exact arts, and the grammar of painting is so much more definite that it makes the difference.

I ought to add, however, that if Mr. Besant says at the beginning of his essay that the 'laws of fiction may be laid down and taught with as much precision and exactness as the laws of harmony, perspective, and proportion,' he mitigates what might appear to be an over-statement by applying his remark to 'general' laws, and by expressing most of these rules in a manner with which it would certainly be unaccommodating to disagree. That the novelist must write from his experience, that his 'characters must be real and such as might be met with in actual life;' that 'a young lady brought up in a quiet country village should avoid descriptions of garrison life,' and 'a writer whose friends and personal experiences belong to the lower middle-class should carefully avoid introducing his characters into Society;' that one should enter one's notes in a common-place book; that one's figures should be clear in outline; that making them clear by some trick of speech or of carriage is a bad method, and 'describing them at length' is a worse one; that English Fiction should have a 'conscious moral purpose;' that 'it is almost impossible to estimate too highly the value of careful workmanship—that is, of style;' that 'the most important point of all is the story,' that 'the story is everything'—these are principles with most of which it is surely impossible not to sympathise. That remark about the lower middle-class writer and his knowing his place is perhaps rather chilling; but for the rest, I should find it difficult to dissent from any one of these recommendations. At the same time I should find it difficult positively to assent to them, with the exception, perhaps, of the injunction as to entering one's notes in a common-place book. They scarcely seem to me to have the quality that Mr. Besant attributes to the rules of the novelist—the 'precision and exactness' of 'the laws of harmony, perspective, and proportion.' They are suggestive, they are even inspiring, but they are not exact, though they are doubtless as much so as the case admits of; which is a proof of that liberty of interpretation for which I just contended. For the value of these different injunctions—so beautiful and so vague—is wholly in the meaning one attaches to them. The characters, the situation, which strike one as real will be those that touch and interest one most, but the measure of reality is very difficult to fix. The reality of Don Quixote or of Mr. Micawber is a very delicate shade; it is a reality so coloured by the author's vision that, vivid as it may be, one would hesitate to propose it as a model; one would expose one's self to some very embarrassing questions on the part of a pupil. It goes without saying that you will not write a good novel unless you possess the sense of reality; but it will be difficult to give you a recipe for calling that sense into being. Humanity is immense and reality has a myriad forms; the most one can affirm is that some of the flowers of fiction have the odour of it, and others have not; as for telling you in advance how your nosegay should be composed, that is another affair. It is equally excellent and inconclusive to say that one must write from experience; to our supposititious aspirant such a declaration might savour of mockery. What kind of experience is intended, and where does it begin and end? Experience is never limited and it is never complete; it is an immense sensibility, a kind of huge spider-web, of the finest silken threads, suspended in the chamber of consciousness and catching every air-borne particle in its tissue. It is the very atmosphere of the mind; and when the mind is imaginative—much more when it happens to be that of a man of genius—it takes to itself the faintest hints of life, it converts the very pulses of the air into revelations. The young lady living in a village has only to be a damsel upon whom nothing is lost to make it quite unfair (as it seems to me) to declare to her that she shall have nothing to say about the military. Greater miracles have been seen than that, imagination assisting, she should speak the truth about some of these gentlemen. I remember an English novelist, a woman of genius, telling me that she was much commended for the impression she had managed to give in one of her tales of the nature and way of life of the French Protestant youth. She had been asked where she learned so much about this recondite being, she had been congratulated on her peculiar opportunities. These opportunities consisted in her having once, in Paris, as she ascended a staircase, passed an open door where, in the household of a *pasteur*, some of the young Protestants were seated at table round a finished meal. The glimpse made a picture; it lasted only a moment, but that moment was experience. She had got her impression, and she evolved her type. She knew what youth was, and what Protestantism; she also had the advantage of having seen what it was to be French; so that she converted these ideas into a concrete image and produced a reality. Above all, however, she was blessed with the faculty which when you give it an inch takes an ell, and which for the artist is a much greater source of strength than any accident of residence or of place in the social scale. The power to guess the unseen from the seen, to trace the implication of things, to judge the whole piece by the pattern, the condition of feeling life, in general, so completely that you are well on your way to knowing any particular corner of it—this cluster of gifts may almost be said to constitute experience, and they occur in country and in town, and in the most differing stages of education. If experience consists of impressions, it may be said that impressions *are* experience, just as (have we not seen it?) they are the very air we breathe. Therefore, if I should certainly say to a novice, 'Write from experience, and experience only,' I should feel that this was a rather tantalising monition if I were not careful immediately to add, 'Try to be one of the people on whom nothing is lost!'

I am far from intending by this to minimise the importance of exactness—of truth of detail. One can speak best from one's own taste, and I may therefore venture to say that the air of reality (solidity of specification) seems to me to be the supreme virtue of a novel—the merit on which all its other merits (including that conscious moral purpose of which Mr. Besant speaks) helplessly and submissively depend. If it be not there, they are all as nothing, and if these be there, they owe their effect to the success with which the author has produced the illusion of life. The cultivation of this success, the study of this exquisite process, form, to my taste, the beginning and the end of the art of the novelist. They are his inspiration, his despair, his reward, his torment, his delight. It is here, in very truth, that he competes with life; it is here that he competes with his brother the painter, in *his* attempt to render the look of things, the look that conveys their meaning, to catch the colour, the relief, the expression, the surface, the substance of the human spectacle. It is in regard to this that Mr. Besant is well inspired when he bids him take notes. He cannot possibly take too many, he cannot possibly take enough. All life solicits him, and to 'render' the simplest surface, to produce the most momentary illusion, is a very complicated business. His case would be easier, and the rule would be more exact, if Mr. Besant had been able to tell him what notes to take. But this I fear he can never learn in any hand-book; it is the business of his life. He has to take a great many in order to select a few, he has to work them up as he can, and even the guides and philosophers who might have most to say to him must leave him alone when it comes to the application of precepts, as we leave the painter in communion with his palette. That his characters 'must be clear in outline,' as Mr. Besant says—he feels that down to his boots; but how he shall make them so is a secret between his good angel and himself. It would be absurdly simple if he could be taught that a great deal of 'description' would make them so, or that, on the contrary, the absence of description and the cultivation of dialogue, or the absence of dialogue and the multiplication of 'incident,' would rescue him from his difficulties. Nothing, for instance, is more possible than that he be of a turn of mind for which this odd, literal opposition of description and dialogue, incident and description, has little meaning and light. People often talk of these things as if they had a kind of internecine distinctness, instead of melting into each other at every breath and being intimately associated parts of one general effort of expression. I cannot imagine composition existing in a series of blocks, nor conceive, in any novel worth discussing at all, of a passage of description that is not in its intention narrative, a passage of dialogue that is not in its intention descriptive, a touch of truth of any sort that does not partake of the nature of incident, and an incident that derives its interest from any other source than the general and only source of the success of a work of art—that of being illustrative. A novel is a living thing, all one and continuous, like every other organism, and in proportion as it lives will it be found, I think, that in each of the parts there is something of each of the other parts. The critic who over the close texture of a finished work will pretend to trace a geography of items will mark some frontiers as artificial, I fear, as any that have been known to history. There is an old-fashioned distinction between the novel of character and the novel of incident, which must have cost many a smile to the intending romancer who was keen about his work. It appears to me as little to the point as the equally celebrated distinction between the novel and the romance—to answer as little to any reality. There are bad novels and good novels, as there are bad pictures and good pictures; but that is the only distinction in which I see any meaning, and I can as little imagine speaking of a novel of character as I can imagine speaking of a picture of character. When one says picture, one says of character, when one says novel, one says of incident, and the terms may be transposed. What is character but the determination of incident? What is incident but the illustration of character? What is a picture or a novel that is *not* of character? What else do we seek in it and find in it? It is an incident for a woman to stand up with her hand resting on a table and look out at you in a certain way; or if it be not an incident, I think it will be hard to say what it is. At the same time it is an expression of character. If you say you don't see it (character in *that—allons donc!*) this is exactly what the artist who has reasons of his own for thinking he *does* see it undertakes to show you. When a young man makes up his mind that he has not faith enough, after all, to enter the Church, as he intended, that is an incident, though you may not hurry to the end of the chapter to see whether perhaps he doesn't change once more. I do not say that these are extraordinary or startling incidents. I do not pretend to estimate the degree of interest proceeding from them, for this will depend upon the skill of the painter. It sounds almost puerile to say that some incidents are intrinsically much more important than others, and I need not take this precaution after having professed my sympathy for the major ones in remarking that the only classification of the novel that I can understand is into the interesting and the uninteresting.

The novel and the romance, the novel of incident and that of character—these separations appear to me to have been made by critics and readers for their own convenience, and to help them out of some of their difficulties, but to have little reality or interest for the producer, from whose point of view it is, of course, that we are attempting to consider the art of fiction. The case is the same with another shadowy category, which Mr. Besant apparently is disposed to set up—that of the 'modern English novel;' unless, indeed, it be that in this matter he has fallen into an accidental confusion of standpoints. It is not quite clear whether he intends the remarks in which he alludes to it to be didactic or historical. It is as difficult to suppose a person intending to write a modern English, as to suppose him writing an ancient English, novel; that is a label which begs the question. One writes the novel, one paints the picture, of one's language and of one's time, and calling it modern English will not, alas! make the difficult task any easier. No more, unfortunately, will calling this or that work of one's fellow artist a romance—unless it be, of course, simply for the pleasantness of the thing, as, for instance, when Hawthorne gave this heading to his story of Blithedale.

The French, who have brought the theory of fiction to remarkable completeness, have but one word for the novel, and have not attempted smaller things in it, that I can see, for that. I can think of no obligation to which the 'romancer' would not be held equally with the novelist; the standard of execution is equally high for each. Of course it is of execution that we are talking—that being the only point of a novel that is open to contention. This is perhaps too often lost sight of, only to produce interminable confusions and cross-purposes. We must grant the artist his subject, his idea, what the French call his *donnée*; our criticism is applied only to what he makes of it. Naturally I do not mean that we are bound to like it or find it interesting: in case we do not our course is perfectly simple—to let it alone. We may believe that of a certain idea even the most sincere novelist can make nothing at all, and the event may perfectly justify our belief; but the failure will have been a failure to execute, and it is in the execution that the fatal weakness is recorded. If we pretend to respect the artist at all we must allow him his freedom of choice, in the face, in particular cases, of innumerable presumptions that the choice will not fructify. Art derives a considerable part of its beneficial exercise from flying in the face of presumptions, and some of the most interesting experiments of which it is capable are hidden in the bosom of common things. Gustave Flaubert has written a story about the devotion of a servant-girl to a parrot, and the production, highly finished as it is, cannot on the whole be called a success. We are perfectly free to find it flat, but I think it might have been interesting; and I, for my part, am extremely glad he should have written it; it is a contribution to our knowledge of what can be done—or what cannot. Ivan Turgénieff has written a tale about a deaf and dumb serf and a lap-dog, and the thing is touching, loving, a little masterpiece. He struck the note of life where Gustave Flaubert missed it—he flew in the face of a presumption and achieved a victory.

Nothing, of course, will ever take the place of the good old fashion of 'liking' a work of art or not liking it; the more improved criticism will not abolish that primitive, that ultimate, test. I mention this to guard myself from the accusation of intimating that the idea, the subject, of a novel or a picture, does not matter. It matters, to my sense, in the highest degree, and if I might put up a prayer it would be that artists should select none but the richest. Some, as I have already hastened to admit, are much more substantial than others, and it would be a happily arranged world in which persons intending to treat them should be exempt from confusions and mistakes. This fortunate condition will arrive only, I fear, on the same day that critics become purged from error. Meanwhile, I repeat, we do not judge the artist with fairness unless we say to him, 'Oh, I grant you your starting-point, because if I did not I should seem to prescribe to you, and heaven forbid I should take that responsibility.

If I pretend to tell you what you must not take, you will call upon me to tell you then what you must take; in which case I shall be nicely caught! Moreover, it isn't till I have accepted your data that I can begin to measure you. I have the standard; I judge you by what you propose, and you must look out for me there. Of course I may not care for your idea at all; I may think it silly, or stale, or unclean; in which case I wash my hands of you altogether. I may content myself with believing that you will not have succeeded in being interesting, but I shall of course not attempt to demonstrate it, and you will be as indifferent to me as I am to you. I needn't remind you that there are all sorts of tastes: who can know it better? Some people, for excellent reasons, don't like to read about carpenters; others, for reasons even better, don't like to read about courtesans. Many object to Americans. Others (I believe they are mainly editors and publishers) won't look at Italians. Some readers don't like quiet subjects; others don't like bustling ones. Some enjoy a complete illusion; others revel in a complete deception. They choose their novels accordingly, and if they don't care about your idea they won't, *a fortiori*, care about your treatment.'

So that it comes back very quickly, as I have said, to the liking; in spite of M. Zola, who reasons less powerfully than he represents, and who will not reconcile himself to this absoluteness of taste, thinking that there are certain things that people ought to like, and that they can be made to like. I am quite at a loss to imagine anything (at any rate in this matter of fiction) that people *ought* to like or to dislike. Selection will be sure to take care of itself, for it has a constant motive behind it. That motive is simply experience. As people feel life, so they will feel the art that is most closely related to it. This closeness of relation is what we should never forget in talking of the effort of the novel. Many people speak of it as a factitious, artificial form, a product of ingenuity, the business of which is to alter and arrange the things that surround us, to translate them into conventional, traditional moulds. This, however, is a view of the matter which carries us but a very short way, condemns the art to an eternal repetition of a few familiar *clichés*, cuts short its development, and leads us straight up to a dead wall. Catching the very note and trick, the strange irregular rhythm of life, that is the attempt whose strenuous force keeps Fiction upon her feet. In proportion as in what she offers us we see life *without* rearrangement do we feel that we are touching the truth; in proportion as we see it *with* rearrangement do we feel that we are being put off with a substitute, a compromise and convention. It is not uncommon to hear an extraordinary assurance of remark in regard to this matter of rearranging, which is often spoken of as if it were the last word of art. Mr. Besant seems to me in danger of falling into this great error with his rather unguarded talk about 'selection.' Art is essentially selection, but it is a selection whose main care is to be typical, to be inclusive. For many people art means rose-coloured windows, and selection means picking a bouquet for Mrs. Grundy. They will tell you glibly that artistic considerations have nothing to do with the disagreeable, with the ugly; they will rattle off shallow commonplaces about the province of art and the limits of art, till you are moved to some wonder in return as to the province and the limits of ignorance. It appears to me that no one can ever have made a seriously artistic attempt without becoming conscious of an immense increase—a kind of revelation—of freedom. One perceives, in that case—by the light of a heavenly ray—that the province of art is all life, all feeling, all observation, all vision. As Mr. Besant so justly intimates, it is all experience. That is a sufficient answer to those who maintain that it must not touch the painful, who stick into its divine unconscious bosom little prohibitory inscriptions on the end of sticks, such as we see in public gardens—'It is forbidden to walk on the grass; it is forbidden to touch the flowers; it is not allowed to introduce dogs, or to remain after dark; it is requested to keep to the right.' The young aspirant in the line of fiction, whom we continue to imagine, will do nothing without taste, for in that case his freedom would be of little use to him; but the first advantage of his taste will be to reveal to him the absurdity of the little sticks and tickets. If he have taste, I must add, of course he will have ingenuity, and my disrespectful reference to that quality just now was not meant to imply that it is useless in fiction. But it is only a secondary aid; the first is a vivid sense of reality.

Mr. Besant has some remarks on the question of 'the story,' which I shall not attempt to criticise, though they seem to me to contain a singular ambiguity, because I do not think I understand them. I cannot see what is meant by talking as if there were a part of a novel which is the story and part of it which for mystical reasons is not—unless indeed the distinction be made in a sense in which it is difficult to suppose that anyone should attempt to convey anything. 'The story,' if it represents anything, represents the subject, the idea, the data of the novel; and there is surely no 'school'—Mr. Besant speaks of a school— which urges that a novel should be all treatment and no subject. There must assuredly be something to treat; every school is intimately conscious of that. This sense of the story being the idea, the starting-point, of the novel is the only one that I see in which it can be spoken of as something different from its organic whole; and since, in proportion as the work is successful, the idea permeates and penetrates it, informs and animates it, so that every word and every punctuation-point contribute directly to the expression, in that proportion do we lose our sense of the story being a blade which may be drawn more or less out of its sheath. The story and the novel, the idea and the form, are the needle and thread, and I never heard of a guild of tailors who recommended the use of the thread without the needle or the needle without the thread. Mr.

Besant is not the only critic who may be observed to have spoken as if there were certain things in life which constitute stories and certain others which do not. I find the same odd implication in an entertaining article in the *Pall Mall Gazette*, devoted, as it happens, to Mr. Besant's lecture. 'The story is the thing!' says this graceful writer, as if with a tone of opposition to another idea. I should think it was, as every painter who, as the time for 'sending in' his picture looms in the distance, finds himself still in quest of a subject—as every belated artist, not fixed about his *donnée*, will heartily agree. There are some subjects which speak to us and others which do not, but he would be a clever man who should undertake to give a rule by which the story and the no-story should be known apart. It is impossible (to me at least) to imagine any such rule which shall not be altogether arbitrary. The writer in the *Pall Mall* opposes the delightful (as I suppose) novel of *Margot la Balafrée* to certain tales in which 'Bostonian nymphs' appear to have 'rejected English dukes for psychological reasons.' I am not acquainted with the romance just designated, and can scarcely forgive the *Pall Mall* critic for not mentioning the name of the author, but the title appears to refer to a lady who may have received a scar in some heroic adventure. I am inconsolable at not being acquainted with this episode, but am utterly at a loss to see why it is a story when the rejection (or acceptance) of a duke is not, and why a reason, psychological or other, is not a subject when a cicatrix is. They are all particles of the multitudinous life with which the novel deals, and surely no dogma which pretends to make it lawful to touch the one and unlawful to touch the other will stand for a moment on its feet. It is the special picture that must stand or fall, according as it seems to possess truth or to lack it. Mr. Besant does not, to my sense, light up the subject by intimating that a story must, under penalty of not being a story, consist of 'adventures.' Why of adventures more than of green spectacles? He mentions a category of impossible things, and among them he places 'fiction without adventure.' Why without adventure, more than without matrimony, or celibacy, or parturition, or cholera, or hydropathy, or Jansenism? This seems to me to bring the novel back to the hapless little *rôle* of being an artificial, ingenious thing—bring it down from its large, free character of an immense and exquisite correspondence with life. And what *is* adventure, when it comes to that, and by what sign is the listening pupil to recognise it? It is an adventure—an immense one—for me to write this little article; and for a Bostonian nymph to reject an English duke is an adventure only less stirring, I should say, than for an English duke to be rejected by a Bostonian nymph. I see dramas within dramas in that, and innumerable points of view. A psychological reason is, to my imagination, an object adorably pictorial; to catch the tint of its complexion—I feel as if that idea might inspire one to Titianesque efforts. There are few things more exciting to me, in short, than a psychological reason, and yet, I protest, the novel seems to me the most magnificent form of art. I have just been reading, at the same time, the delightful story of *Treasure Island*, by Mr. Robert Louis Stevenson, and the last tale from M. Edmond de Goncourt, which is entitled *Chérie*. One of these works treats of murders, mysteries, islands of dreadful renown, hairbreadth escapes, miraculous coincidences and buried doubloons. The other treats of a little French girl who lived in a fine house in Paris and died of wounded sensibility because no one would marry her. I call *Treasure Island* delightful, because it appears to me to have succeeded wonderfully in what it attempts; and I venture to bestow no epithet upon *Chérie*, which strikes me as having failed in what it attempts—that is, in tracing the development of the moral consciousness of a child. But one of these productions strikes me as exactly as much of a novel as the other, and as having a 'story' quite as much. The moral consciousness of a child is as much a part of life as the islands of the Spanish Main, and the one sort of geography seems to me to have those 'surprises' of which Mr. Besant speaks quite as much as the other. For myself (since it comes back in the last resort, as I say, to the preference of the individual), the picture of the child's experience has the advantage that I can at successive steps (an immense luxury, near to the 'sensual pleasure' of which Mr. Besant's critic in the *Pall Mall* speaks) say Yes or No, as it may be, to what the artist puts before me. I have been a child, but I have never been on a quest for a

HENRY JAMES
BY JOHN S. SARGENT

From a drawing done in 1886, and reproduced
in *The Yellow Book*, Vol. 2, July, 1894

buried treasure, and it is a simple accident that with M. de Goncourt I should have for the most part to say No. With George Eliot, when she painted that country, I always said Yes.

The most interesting part of Mr. Besant's lecture is unfortunately the briefest passage—his very cursory allusion to the 'conscious moral purpose' of the novel. Here again it is not very clear whether he is recording a fact or laying down a principle; it is a great pity that in the latter case he should not have developed his idea. This branch of the subject is of immense importance, and Mr. Besant's few words point to considerations of the widest reach, not to be lightly disposed of. He will have treated the art of fiction but superficially who is not prepared to go every inch of the way that these considerations will carry him. It is for this reason that at the beginning of these remarks I was careful to notify the reader that my reflections on so large a theme have no pretension to be exhaustive. Like Mr. Besant, I have left the question of the morality of the novel till the last, and at the last I find I have used up my space. It is a question surrounded with difficulties, as witness the very first that meets us, in the form of a definite question, on the threshold. Vagueness, in such a discussion, is fatal, and what is the meaning of your morality and your conscious moral purpose? Will you not define your terms and explain how (a novel being a picture) a picture can be either moral or immoral? You wish to paint a moral picture or carve a moral statue; will you not tell us how you would set about it? We are discussing the Art of Fiction; questions of art are questions (in the widest sense) of execution; questions of morality are quite another affair, and will you not let us see how it is that you find it so easy to mix them up? These things are so clear to Mr. Besant that he has deduced from them a law which he sees embodied in English Fiction and which is 'a truly admirable thing and a great cause for congratulation.' It is a great cause for congratulation, indeed, when such thorny problems become as smooth as silk. I may add that, in so far as Mr. Besant perceives that in point of fact English Fiction has addressed itself preponderantly to these delicate questions, he will appear to many people to have made a vain discovery. They will have been positively struck, on the contrary, with the moral timidity of the usual English novelist; with his (or with her) aversion to face the difficulties with which, on every side, the treatment of reality bristles. He is apt to be extremely shy (whereas the picture that Mr. Besant draws is a picture of boldness), and the sign of his work, for the most part, is a cautious silence on certain subjects. In the English novel (by which I mean the American as well), more than in any other, there is a traditional difference between that which people know and that which they agree to admit that they know, that which they see and that which they speak of, that which they feel to be a part of life and that which they allow to enter into literature. There is the great difference, in short, between what they talk of in conversation and what they talk of in print. The essence of moral energy is to survey the whole field, and I should directly reverse Mr. Besant's remark, and say not that the English novel has a purpose, but that it has a diffidence. To what degree a purpose in a work of art is a source of corruption I shall not attempt to inquire; the one that seems to me least dangerous is the purpose of making a perfect work. As for our novel, I may say, lastly, on this score, that, as we find it in England to-day, it strikes me as addressed in a large degree to 'young people,' and that this in itself constitutes a presumption that it will be rather shy. There are certain things which it is generally agreed not to discuss, not even to mention, before young people. That is very well, but the absence of discussion is not a symptom of the moral passion. The purpose of the English novel—'a truly admirable thing, and a great cause for congratulation'—strikes me, therefore, as rather negative.

There is one point at which the moral sense and the artistic sense lie very near together; that is, in the light of the very obvious truth that the deepest quality of a work of art will always be the quality of the mind of the producer. In proportion as that mind is rich and noble will the novel, the picture, the statue, partake of the substance of beauty and truth. To be constituted of such elements is, to my vision, to have purpose enough. No good novel will ever proceed from a superficial mind; that seems to me an axiom which, for the artist in fiction, will cover all needful moral ground; if the youthful aspirant take it to heart it will illuminate for him many of the mysteries of 'purpose.' There are many other useful things that might be said to him, but I have come to the end of my article, and can only touch them as I pass. The critic in the *Pall Mall Gazette*, whom I have already quoted, draws attention to the danger, in speaking of the art of fiction, of generalizing. The danger that he has in mind is rather, I imagine, that of particularizing, for there are some comprehensive remarks which, in addition to those embodied in Mr. Besant's suggestive lecture, might, without fear of misleading him, be addressed to the ingenuous student. I should remind him first of the magnificence of the form that is open to him, which offers to sight so few restrictions and such innumerable opportunities. The other arts, in comparison, appear confined and hampered; the various conditions under which they are exercised are so rigid and definite. But the only condition that I can think of attaching to the composition of the novel is, as I have already said, that it be interesting. This freedom is a splendid privilege, and the first lesson of the young novelist is to learn to be worthy of it. 'Enjoy it as it deserves,' I should say to him; 'take possession of it, explore it to its utmost extent, reveal it, rejoice in it. All life belongs to you, and don't listen either to those who would shut you up into corners of it and tell you that it is only here and there that art inhabits, or to those who would persuade you that this heavenly messenger wings her way outside of life altogether, breathing a superfine air and turning away her head from the truth of things. There is no impression of life, no manner of seeing it and feeling it, to which the plan of the novelist may not offer a place; you have only to remember that talents so dissimilar as those of Alexandre Dumas and Jane Austen, Charles Dickens and Gustave Flaubert, have worked in this field with equal glory. Don't think too much about optimism and pessimism; try and catch the colour of life itself. In France to-day we see a prodigious effort (that of Emile Zola, to whose solid and serious work no explorer of the capacity of the novel can allude without respect), we see an extraordinary effort vitiated by a spirit of pessimism on a narrow basis. M. Zola is magnificent, but he strikes an English reader as ignorant; he has an air of working in the dark; if he had as much light as energy his results would be of the highest value. As for the aberrations of a shallow optimism, the ground (of English fiction especially) is strewn with their brittle particles as with broken glass. If you must indulge in conclusions let them have the taste of a wide knowledge. Remember that your first duty is to be as complete as possible—to make as perfect a work. Be generous and delicate, and then, in the vulgar phrase, go in!'

2

A HUMBLE REMONSTRANCE*

BY ROBERT LOUIS STEVENSON

WE have recently enjoyed a quite peculiar pleasure: hearing, in some detail, the opinions about the art they practise of Mr. Walter Besant and Mr. Henry James; two men certainly of very different calibre: Mr. James so precise of outline, so cunning of fence, so scrupulous of finish, and Mr. Besant so genial, so friendly, with so persuasive and humorous a vein of whim: Mr. James the very type of the deliberate artist, Mr. Besant the impersonation of good nature. That such doctors should differ will excite no great surprise; but one point in which they seem to agree fills me, I confess, with wonder. For they are both content to talk about the 'art of fiction;' and Mr. Besant, waxing exceedingly bold, goes on to oppose this so-called 'art of fiction' to the 'art of poetry.' By the art of poetry he can mean nothing but the art of verse, an art of handicraft, and only comparable with the art of prose. For that heat and height of sane emotion which we agree to call by the name of poetry, is but a libertine and vagrant quality; present, at times, in any art, more often absent from them all; too seldom present in the prose novel, too frequently absent from the ode and epic. Fiction is in the same case;

* Published in *Longman's Magazine*, December 1884, and reprinted in *Memories and Portraits* (1887).

it is no substantive art, but an element which enters largely into all the arts but architecture. Homer, Wordsworth, Phidias, Hogarth, and Salvini, all deal in fiction; and yet I do not suppose that either Hogarth or Salvini, to mention but these two, entered in any degree into the scope of Mr. Besant's interesting lecture or Mr. James's charming essay. The art of fiction, then, regarded as a definition, is both too ample and too scanty. Let me suggest another; let me suggest that what both Mr. James and Mr. Besant had in view was neither more nor less than the art of narrative.

But Mr. Besant is anxious to speak solely of 'the modern English novel,' the stay and bread-winner of Mr. Mudie; and in the author of the most pleasing novel on that roll, *All Sorts and Conditions of Men*, the desire is natural enough. I can conceive then, that he would hasten to propose two additions, and read thus: the art of *fictitious* narrative *in prose*.

Now the fact of the existence of the modern English novel is not to be denied; materially, with its three volumes, leaded type, and gilded lettering, it is easily distinguishable from other forms of literature; but to talk at all fruitfully of any branch of art, it is needful to build our definitions on some more fundamental ground than binding. Why, then, are we to add 'in prose'? *The Odyssey* appears to me among the best of romances; *The Lady of the Lake* to stand high in the second order; and Chaucer's tales and prologues to contain more of the matter and art of the modern English novel than the whole treasury of Mr. Mudie. Whether a narrative be written in blank verse or the Spenserian stanza, in the long period of Gibbon or the chipped phrase of Charles Reade, the principles of the art of narrative must be equally observed. The choice of a noble and swelling style in prose affects the problem of narration in the same way, if not to the same degree, as the choice of measured verse; for both imply a closer synthesis of events, a higher key of dialogue, and a more picked and stately strain of words. If you are to refuse *Don Juan*, it is hard to see why you should include *Zanoni* or (to bracket works of very different value) *The Scarlet Letter*; and by what discrimination are you to open your doors to *The Pilgrim's Progress* and close them on *The Faery Queen*? To bring things closer home, I will here propound to Mr. Besant a conundrum. A narrative called *Paradise Lost* was written in English verse by one John Milton; what was it then? It was next translated by Chateaubriand into French prose; and what was it then? Lastly, the French translation was, by some inspired compatriot of George Gilfillan (and of mine), turned bodily into an English novel; and, in the name of clearness, what was it then?

But, once more, why should we add 'fictitious'? The reason why is obvious. The reason why not, if something more recondite, does not want for weight. The art of narrative, in fact, is the same, whether it is applied to the selection and illustration of a real series of events or of an imaginary series. Boswell's *Life of Johnson* (a work of cunning and inimitable art) owes its success to the same technical manœuvres as (let us say) *Tom Jones*: the clear conception of certain characters of man, the choice and presentation of certain incidents out of a great number that offered, and the invention (yes, invention) and preservation of a certain key in dialogue. In which these things are done with the more art—in which with the greater air of nature—readers will differently judge. Boswell's is, indeed, a very special case, and almost a generic; but it is not only in Boswell, it is in every biography with any salt of life, it is in every history where events and men, rather than ideas, are presented—in Tacitus, in Carlyle, in Michelet, in Macaulay—that the novelist will find many of his own methods most conspicuously and adroitly handled. He will find besides that he, who is free—who has the right to invent or steal a missing incident, who has the right, more precious still, of wholesale omission—is frequently defeated, and, with all his advantages, leaves a less strong impression of reality and passion. Mr. James utters his mind with a becoming fervour on the sanctity of truth to the novelist; on a more careful examination truth will seem a word of very debateable propriety, not only for the labours of the novelist, but for those of the historian. No art—to use the daring phrase of Mr. James—can successfully 'compete with life'; and the art that does so is condemned to perish *montibus aviis*. Life goes before us, infinite in complication; attended by the most various and surprising meteors; appealing at once to the eye, to the ear, to the mind—the seat of wonder, to the touch—so thrillingly delicate, and to the belly—so imperious when starved. It combines and employs in its manifestation the method and material, not of one art only, but of all the arts. Music is but an arbitrary trifling with a few of life's majestic chords; painting is but a shadow of its gorgeous pageantry of light and colour; literature does but drily indicate that wealth of incident, of moral obligation, of virtue, vice, action, rapture, and agony, with which it teems. To 'compete with life,' whose sun we cannot look upon, whose passions and diseases waste and slay us—to compete with the flavour of wine, the beauty of the dawn, the scorching of fire, the bitterness of death and separation—here is, indeed, a projected escalade of heaven; here are, indeed, labours for a Hercules in a dress coat, armed with a pen and a dictionary to depict the passions, armed with a tube of superior flake-white to paint the portrait of the insufferable sun. No art is true in this sense: none can 'compete with life': not even history, built indeed of indisputable facts, but these facts robbed of their vivacity and sting; so that even when we read of the sack of a city or the fall of an empire, we are surprised, and justly commend the author's talent, if our pulse be quickened. And mark, for a last differentia, that this quickening of the pulse is, in almost every case, purely agreeable; that these phantom reproductions of experience, even at their most acute, convey decided pleasure; while experience itself, in the cockpit of life, can torture and slay.

What, then, is the object, what the method, of an art, and what the source of its power? The whole secret is that no art does 'compete with life.' Man's one method, whether he reasons or creates, is to half-shut his eyes against the dazzle and confusion of reality. The arts, like arithmetic and geometry, turn away their eyes from the gross, coloured, and mobile nature at our feet, and regard instead a certain figmentary abstraction. Geometry will tell us of a circle, a thing never seen in nature; asked about a green circle or an iron circle, it lays its hand upon its mouth. So with the arts. Painting, ruefully comparing sunshine and flake-white, gives up truth of colour, as it had already given up relief and movement; and instead of vying with nature, arranges a scheme of harmonious tints. Literature, above all in its most typical mood, the mood of narrative, similarly flees the direct challenge and pursues instead an independent and creative aim. So far as it imitates at all, it imitates not life but speech: not the facts of human destiny, but the emphasis and the suppressions with which the human actor tells of them. The real art that dealt with life directly was that of the first men who told their stories round the savage camp-fire. Our art is occupied, and bound to be occupied, not so much in making stories true as in making them typical; not so much in capturing the lineaments of each fact, as in marshalling all of them towards a common-end. For the welter of impressions, all forcible but all discrete, which life presents, it substitutes a certain artificial series of impressions, all indeed most feebly represented, but all aiming at the same effect, all eloquent of the same idea, all chiming together like consonant notes in music or like the graduated tints in a good picture. From all its chapters, from all its pages, from all its sentences, the well-written novel echoes and re-echoes its one creative and controlling thought; to this must every incident and character contribute; the style must have been pitched in unison with this; and if there is anywhere a word that looks another way, the book would be stronger, clearer, and (I had almost said) fuller without it. Life is monstrous, infinite, illogical, abrupt, and poignant; a work of art, in comparison, is neat, finite, self-contained, rational, flowing, and emasculate. Life imposes by brute energy, like inarticulate thunder; art catches the ear, among the far louder noises of experience like an air artificially made by a discreet musician. A proposition of geometry does not compete with life; and a proposition of geometry is a fair and luminous parallel for a work of art. Both are reasonable, both untrue to the crude fact; both inhere in nature, neither represents it. The novel which is a work of art exists, not by its resemblances to life, which are forced and material, as a shoe must still consist of leather, but by its immeasurable difference from life, which is designed and significant, and is both the method and the meaning of the work.

The life of man is not the subject of novels, but the inexhaustible magazine from which subjects are to be selected; the name of these is legion; and with each new subject—for here again I must differ by the whole width of heaven from Mr. James—the true artist will vary his method and change the point of attack. That which was in one case an excellence, will become a defect in another; what was the making of one book, will in the next be impertinent or dull. First each novel, and then each class of novels, exists by and for itself. I will take, for instance, three main classes, which are fairly distinct: first, the novel of adventure, which appeals to certain almost sensual and quite illogical tendencies in man; second, the novel of character, which appeals to our intellectual appreciation of man's foibles and mingled and inconstant motives; and third, the dramatic novel, which deals with the same stuff as the serious theatre, and appeals to our emotional nature and moral judgment.

And first for the novel of adventure. Mr. James refers, with singular generosity of praise, to a little book about a quest for hidden treasure; but he lets fall, by the way, some rather startling words. In this book he misses what he calls the 'immense luxury' of being able to quarrel with his author. The luxury, to most of us, is to lay by our judgment, to be submerged by the tale as by a billow, and only to awake, and begin to distinguish and find fault, when the piece is over and the volume laid aside. Still more remarkable is Mr. James's reason. He cannot criticise the author, as he goes, 'because,' says he, comparing it with another work, '*I have been a child, but I have never been on a quest for buried treasure.*' Here is, indeed, a wilful paradox; for if he has never been on a quest for buried treasure, it can be demonstrated that he has never been a child. There never was a child (unless Master James) but has hunted gold, and been a pirate, and a military commander, and a bandit of the mountains; but has fought, and suffered shipwreck and prison, and imbrued its little hands in gore, and gallantly retrieved the lost battle, and triumphantly protected innocence and beauty. Elsewhere in his essay Mr. James has protested with excellent reason against too narrow a conception of experience; for the born artist, he contends, the 'faintest hints of life' are converted into revelations; and it will be found true, I believe, in a majority of cases, that the artist writes with more gusto and effect of those things which he has only wished to do, than of those which he has done. Desire is a wonderful telescope, and Pisgah the best observatory. Now, while it is true that neither Mr. James nor the author of the work in question has ever, in the fleshly sense, gone questing after gold, it is probable that both have ardently desired and fondly imagined the details of such a life in youthful day-dreams; and the author, counting upon that, and well aware (cunning and low-minded man!) that this class of interest, having been frequently treated, finds a readily accessible and beaten road to the sympathies of the reader, addressed himself throughout to the building up and circumstantiation of this boyish dream. Character to the boy is a sealed book; for him, a pirate is a beard in wide trousers and literally bristling with pistols. The author, for the sake of circumstantiation and because he was himself more or less grown up, admitted character, within certain limits, into his design; but only within certain limits. Had the same puppets figured in a scheme of another sort, they had been drawn to very different purpose; for in this elementary novel of adventure, the characters need to be presented with but one class of qualities—the warlike and formidable. So as they appear insidious in deceit and fatal in the combat, they have served their end. Danger is the matter with which this class of novel deals; fear, the passion with which it idly trifles; and the characters are portrayed only so far as they realise the sense of danger and provoke the sympathy of fear. To add more traits, to be too clever, to start the hare of moral or intellectual interest while we are running the fox of material interest, is not to enrich but to stultify your tale. The stupid reader will only be offended, and the clever reader lose the scent.

The novel of character has this difference from all others: that it requires no coherency of plot, and for this reason, as in the case of *Gil Blas*, it is sometimes called the novel of adventure. It turns on the humours of the persons represented; these are, to be sure, embodied in incidents, but the incidents themselves, being tributary, need not march in a progression; and the characters may be statically shown. As they enter, so they may go out; they must be consistent, but they need not grow. Here Mr. James will recognise the note of much of his own work: he treats, for the most part, the statics of character, studying it at rest or only gently moved; and, with his usual delicate and just artistic instinct, he avoids those stronger passions which would deform the attitudes he loves to study, and change his sitters from the humourists of ordinary life to the brute forces and bare types of more emotional moments. In his recent *Author of Beltraffio*, so just in conception, so nimble and neat in workmanship, strong passion is indeed employed; but observe that it is not displayed. Even in the heroine the working of the passion is suppressed; and the great struggle, the true tragedy, the *scène-à-faire*, passes unseen behind the panels of a locked door. The delectable invention of the young visitor is introduced, consciously or not, to this end: that Mr. James, true to his method, might avoid the scene of passion. I trust no reader will suppose me guilty of undervaluing this little masterpiece. I mean merely that it belongs to one marked class of novel, and that it would have been very differently conceived and treated had it belonged to that other marked class, of which I now proceed to speak.

I take pleasure in calling the dramatic novel by that name, because it enables me to point out by the way a strange and peculiarly English misconception. It is sometimes supposed that the drama consists of incident. It

ROBERT LOUIS STEVENSON
BY JOHN S. SARGENT

The second of Sargent's two portraits of Stevenson, painted at Bournemouth in the summer of 1885. The first had been done towards the end of the previous year.

' Sargent was down again and painted a portrait of me walking about in my own dining-room, in my own velveteen jacket, and twisting as I go my own moustache; at one corner a glimpse of my wife, in an Indian dress, and seated in a chair that was once my grandfather's—but since some months goes by the name of Henry James's, for it was there the novelist loved to sit—adds a touch of poesy and comicality. It is, I think, excellent, but is too eccentric to be exhibited. I am at one extreme corner; my wife, in this wild dress, and looking like a ghost, is at the extreme other end; between us an open door exhibits my palatial entrance hall and a part of my respected staircase. All this is touched in lovely, with that witty touch of Sargent's; but of course, it looks dam queer as a whole.' *Letter to W. H. Low, October 22, 1885.*

consists of passion, which gives the actor his opportunity; and that passion must progressively increase, or the actor, as the piece proceeded, would be unable to carry the audience from a lower to a higher pitch of interest and emotion. A good serious play must therefore be founded on one of the passionate *cruces* of life, where duty and inclination come nobly to the grapple; and the same is true of what I call, for that reason, the dramatic novel. I will instance a few worthy specimens, all of our own day and language: Meredith's *Rhoda Fleming*, that wonderful and painful book, long out of print and hunted for at bookstalls like an Aldine; Hardy's *Pair of Blue Eyes*; and two of Charles Reade's, *Griffith Gaunt* and *The Double Marriage*, originally called *White Lies* and founded (by an accident quaintly favourable to my nomenclature) on a play by Maquet, the partner of the great Dumas. In this kind of novel the closed door of *The Author of Beltraffio* must be broken open; passion must appear upon the scene and utter its last word; passion is the be-all and the end-all, the plot and the solution, the protagonist and the *deus ex machinâ* in one. The characters may come anyhow upon the stage: we do not care; the point is, that, before they leave it, they shall become transfigured and raised out of themselves by passion. It may be part of the design to draw them with detail; to depict a full-length character, and then behold it melt and change in the furnace of emotion. But there is no obligation of the sort; nice portraiture is not required; and we are content to accept mere abstract types, so they be strongly and sincerely moved. A novel of this class may be even great, and yet contain no individual figure; it may be great, because it displays the workings of the perturbed heart and the impersonal utterance of passion; and with an artist of the second class it is, indeed, even more likely to be great, when the issue has thus been narrowed and the whole force of the writer's mind directed to passion alone. Cleverness again, which has its fair field in the novel of character, is debarred all entry upon this more solemn theatre. A far-fetched motive, an ingenious evasion of the issue, a witty instead of a passionate turn, offend us like an insincerity. All should be plain, all straightforward to the end. Hence it is that, in *Rhoda Fleming*, Mrs. Lovel raises such resentment in the reader; her motives are too flimsy, her ways are too equivocal, for the weight and strength of her surroundings. Hence the hot indignation of the reader when Balzac, after having begun the *Duchesse de Langeais* in terms of strong if somewhat swollen passion, cuts the knot by the derangement of the hero's clock. Such personages and incidents belong to the novel of character; they are out of place in the high society of the passions; when the passions are introduced in art at their full height, we look to see them, not baffled and impotently striving, as in life, but towering above circumstance and acting substitutes for fate.

And here I can imagine Mr. James, with his lucid sense, to intervene. To much of what I have said he would apparently demur; in much he would, somewhat impatiently, acquiesce. It may be true; but it is not what he desired to say or to hear said. He spoke of the finished picture and its worth when done; I, of the brushes, the palette, and the north light. He uttered his views in the tone and for the ear of good society; I, with the emphasis and technicalities of the obtrusive student. But the point, I may reply, is not merely to amuse the public, but to offer helpful advice to the young writer. And the young writer will not so much be helped by genial pictures of what an art may aspire to at its highest, as by a true idea of what it must be on the lowest terms. The best that we can say to him is this: Let him choose a motive, whether of character or passion; carefully construct his plot so that every incident is an illustration of the motive and every property employed shall bear to it a near relation of congruity or contrast; avoid a sub-plot, unless, as sometimes in Shakespeare, the sub-plot be a reversion or complement of the main intrigue; suffer not his style to flag below the level of the argument; pitch the key of conversation, not with any thought of how men talk in parlours, but with a single eye to the degree of passion he may be called on to express; and allow neither himself in the narrative nor any character in the course of the dialogue, to utter one sentence that is not part and parcel of the business of the story or the discussion of the problem involved. Let him not regret if this shortens his book; it will be better so; for to add irrelevant matter is not to lengthen but to bury. Let him not mind if he miss a thousand qualities, so that he keeps unflaggingly in pursuit of the one he has chosen. Let him not care particularly if he miss the tone of conversation, the pungent material detail of the day's manners, the reproduction of the atmosphere and the environment. These elements are not essential: a novel may be excellent, and yet have none of them; a passion or a character is so much the better depicted as it rises clearer from material circumstance. In this age of the particular, let him remember the ages of the abstract, the great books of the past, the brave men that lived before Shakespeare and before Balzac. And as the root of the whole matter, let him bear in mind that his novel is not a transcript of life, to be judged by its exactitude; but a simplification of some side or point of life, to stand or fall by its significant simplicity. For although, in great men, working upon great motives, what we observe and admire is often their complexity, yet underneath appearances the truth remains unchanged: that simplification was their method, and that simplicity is their excellence.

3

JAMES TO STEVENSON

3 Bolton St., W.
December 5th [1884]

MY DEAR ROBERT LOUIS STEVENSON,

I read only last night your paper in the December *Longman's* in genial rejoinder to my article in the same periodical on Besant's lecture, and the result of that charming half-hour is a friendly desire to send you three words. Not words of discussion, dissent, retort or remonstrance, but of hearty sympathy, charged with the assurance of my enjoyment of everything you write. It's a luxury, in this immoral age, to encounter some one who *does* write—who is really acquainted with that lovely art. It wouldn't be fair to contend with you here; besides, we agree, I think, much more than we disagree, and though there are points as to which a more irrepressible spirit than mine would like to try a fall, that is not what I want to say—but on the contrary, to thank you for so much that is suggestive and felicitous in your remarks—justly felt and brilliantly said. They are full of these things, and the current of your admirable style floats pearls and diamonds. Excellent are your closing words, and no one can assent more than I to your proposition that all art is a simplification. It is a pleasure to see that truth so neatly uttered. My pages, in *Longman*, were simply a plea for liberty: they were only half of what I had to say, and some day I shall try and express the remainder. Then I shall tickle you a little affectionately as I pass. You will say that my 'liberty' is an obese divinity, requiring extra measures; but after one more go I shall hold my tongue. The native *gaiety* of all that you write is delightful to me, and when I reflect that it proceeds from a man whom life has laid much of the time on his back (as I understand it), I find you a genius indeed. There must be pleasure in it for you too. I ask Colvin about you whenever I see him, and I shall have to send him this to forward to you. I am with innumerable good wishes yours very faithfully,

HENRY JAMES.

4

STEVENSON TO JAMES

Bonallie Towers, Branksome Park,
Bournemouth, December 8*th*, 1884

MY DEAR HENRY JAMES,

This is a very brave hearing from more points than one. The first point is that there is a hope of a sequel. For this I laboured. Seriously, from the dearth of information and thoughtful interest in the art of literature, those who try to practise it with any deliberate purpose run the risk of finding no fit audience. People suppose it is 'the stuff' that interests them; they think, for instance, that the prodigious fine thoughts and sentiments in Shakespeare impress by their own weight, not understanding that the unpolished diamond is but a stone. They think that striking situations, or good dialogue, are got by studying life; they will not rise to understand that they are prepared by deliberate artifice and set off by painful suppressions. Now, I want the whole thing well ventilated, for my own education and the public's, and I beg you to look as quick as you can, to follow me up with every circumstance of defeat where we differ, and (to prevent the flouting of the laity) to emphasise the points where we agree. I trust your paper will show me the way to a rejoinder; and that rejoinder I shall hope to make with so much art as to woo or drive you from your threatened silence. I would not ask better than to pass my life in beating out this quarter of corn with such a seconder as yourself.

Point the second—I am rejoiced indeed to hear you speak so kindly of my work; rejoiced and surprised. I seem to myself a very rude, left-handed countryman; not fit to be read, far less complimented, by a man so accomplished, so adroit, so craftsmanlike as you. You will happily never have cause to understand the despair with which a writer like myself considers (say) the park scene in *Lady Barberina*. Every touch surprises me by its intangible precision; and the effect when done, as light as syllabub, as distinct as a picture, fills me with envy. Each man among us prefers his own aim, and I prefer mine; but when we come to speak of performance, I recognise myself, compared with you, to be a lout and slouch of the first water.

Where we differ, both as to the design of stories and the delineation of character, I begin to lament. Of course, I am not so dull as to ask you to desert your walk; but could you not, in one novel, to oblige a sincere admirer, and to enrich his shelves with a beloved volume, <u>could you not, and might you not, cast your characters in a mould a little more abstract and academic</u> (dear Mrs. Pennyman* had already, among your other work, a taste of what I mean), <u>and pitch the incidents, I do not say in any stronger, but in a slightly more emphatic key</u>—as it were an episode from one of the old (so-called) novels of adventure? I fear you will not; and I suppose I must sighingly admit you to be right. And yet, when I see, as it were, a book of *Tom Jones* handled with your exquisite precision and shot through with those sidelights of reflection in which you excel, I relinquish the dear vision with regret. Think upon it.

As you know, I belong to that besotted class of man, the invalid: this puts me to a stand in the way of visits. But it is possible that some day you may feel that a day near the sea and among pinewoods would be a pleasant change from town. If so, please let us know; and my wife and I will be delighted to put you up, and give you what

* A character in James's *Washington Square* (actually Penniman).

we can to eat and drink (I have a fair bottle of claret).—
On the back of which, believe me, yours sincerely,

ROBERT LOUIS STEVENSON.

P.S. I reopen this to say that I have re-read my paper, and cannot think I have at all succeeded in being either veracious or polite. I knew, of course, that I took your paper merely as a pin to hang my own remarks upon; but, alas! what a thing is any paper! What fine remarks can you not hang on mine! How I have sinned against proportion, and with every effort to the contrary, against the merest rudiments of courtesy to you! You are indeed a very acute reader to have divined the real attitude of my mind; and I can only conclude, not without closed eyes and shrinking shoulders, in the well-worn words,

Lay on, Macduff!

5

STEVENSON TO JAMES*

Skerryvore, Bournemouth, October 28th, 1885

MY DEAR HENRY JAMES,

At last, my wife being at a concert, and a story being done, I am at some liberty to write and give you of my

* James and Stevenson had met at Bournemouth early in 1885, and James was by now a familiar and welcome guest at Skerryvore with a special chair kept for him at the fireside.

views. And first, many thanks for the works that came to my sickbed. And second, and more important, as to *The Princess*.* Well, I think you are going to do it this time; I cannot, of course, foresee, but these two first numbers seem to me picturesque and sound and full of lineament, and very much a new departure. As for your young lady, she is all there; yes, sir, you can do low life, I believe. The prison was excellent; it was of that nature of touch that I sometimes achingly miss from your former work: with some of the grime, that is, and some of the emphasis of skeleton there is in nature. I pray you to take grime in a good sense; it need not be ignoble; dirt may have dignity; in nature it usually has; and your prison was imposing.

And now to the main point; why do we not see you? Do not fail us. Make an alarming sacrifice, and let us see 'Henry James's chair' properly occupied. I never sit in it myself (though it was my grandfather's); it has been consecrated to guests by your approval, and now stands at my elbow gaping. We have a new room, too, to introduce to you—our last baby, the drawing-room; it never cries, and has cut its teeth. Likewise, there is a cat now. It promises to be a monster of laziness and self-sufficiency.

Pray see, in the November *Time* (a dread name for a magazine of light reading), a very clever fellow, W.

---

* *The Princess Casamassima* appeared as a serial in the *Atlantic Monthly* from September 1885 to October 1886.

Archer, stating his views of me;* the rosy-gilled 'athletico-æsthete'; and warning me, in a fatherly manner, that a rheumatic fever would try my philosophy (as indeed it would), and that my gospel would not do for 'those who are shut out from the exercise of any manly virtue save renunciation.' To those who know that rickety and cloistered spectre, the real R. L. S., the paper, besides being clever in itself, presents rare elements of sport. The critical parts are in particular very bright and neat, and often excellently true. Get it by all manner of means.

I hear on all sides I am to be attacked as an immoral writer; this is painful. Have I at last got, like you, to the pitch of being attacked? 'Tis the consecration I lack—and could do without. Not that Archer's paper is an attack, or what either he or I, I believe, would call one; 'tis the attacks on my morality (which I had thought a gem of the first water) I referred to.

Now, my dear James, come—come—come. The spirit (that is me) says, Come; and the bride (and that is my wife) says, Come; and the best thing you can do for us and yourself and your work is to get up and do so right away.

Yours affectionately,
ROBERT LOUIS STEVENSON.

---

* 'R. L. Stevenson: his Style and Thought.'

6

HENRY JAMES*

Who comes to-night? We ope the doors in vain.
Who comes? My bursting walls, can you contain
The presences that now together throng
Your narrow entry, as with flowers and song,
As with the air of life, the breath of talk?
Lo, how these fair immaculate women walk
Behind their jocund maker; and we see
Slighted *De Mauves*, and that far different she,
Gressie, the trivial sphynx; and to our feast
Daisy and *Barb* and *Chancellor* (she not least!)
With all their silken, all their airy kin,
Do like unbidden angels enter in.
But he, attended by these shining names,
Comes (best of all) himself—our welcome James.

* This poem was written by Stevenson in 1885 and published in *Underwoods* (1887). The names in italics are those of the heroines of James's stories, *Madame de Mauves*, *Georgina's Reasons*, *Daisy Miller*, *Lady Barberina*, and *The Bostonians*.

the modest hen canary, I can only attempt
to express my thanks in plain prose.

[sketch of five framed pictures arranged on a wall]

The above, as you will easily perceive, is
the present aspect of the side wall of our
sitting room. corrects and carefully drawn.
with Taylor's beautiful work. Our Lemons
lovable picture of horses, the magic
river, Sargent's picture of Iris, and the
ivy of Chatterton.

At this stage, my wife was (as
should have been) removed to an asylum.
have not fallen quite so low, for
I reserve my vases. When they go, you
will know that Stevenson lies cold

and ourselves, and the mirror represents us, the walls and furniture. I seem to be topsy-turvey in June. Buxton is no doubt gone are a fine fellows and Stevenson loves. Have, when the house shall continue. contentive a thousand thanks from

Yours affectionately
†(the) R.Lewhtkins Stevenson

† you see my state of idiocy; I began to sign this "Henry James": the exphon James for me
R.L.S.

7

THE STEVENSONS TO JAMES*

Skerryvore, Bournemouth [*February 25th*, 1886]

MY DEAR MR. JAMES,

A magic mirror has come to us which seems to reflect not only our own plain faces, but the kindly one of a friend entwined in the midst of all sorts of pleasant memories. Louis felt that verse alone would fitly convey his sentiments concerning this beautiful present, but his muse, I believe, has not as yet responded to his call. As for me, to whom the gift of song has been denied in common with the modest hen canary, I can only attempt to express my thanks in plain prose.

[*Here follows a sketch showing four pictures set round a square mirror with a carved frame.*]

The above, as you will easily perceive, is the present aspect of the side wall of our drawing room, correctly and carefully drawn. Miss Taylor's beautiful work, Mr. Lemon's adorable picture of horses, the magic mirror, Sargent's picture of Louis, and the copy of Chatterton.

At this stage, my wife was (or should have been) removed to an asylum. I have not fallen quite so low, for I

---

* The first part of this letter, down to 'Chatterton', is in Fanny Stevenson's handwriting; the rest in Stevenson's.

reserve my verses. When they go, you will know that Skerryvore lies cold and smokeless, and the mirror represents only the walls and furniture. I scorn to try to express myself in prose. But there is no doubt you are a fine fellow and the mirror lovely. More, when the Muse shall countenance, and meantime a thousand thanks from
Yours affectionately,
† (Hen) Robert Louis Stevenson

† You see my state of idiocy: I began to sign this "Henry James": The asylum yawns for me.
R.L.S.

8

STEVENSON TO JAMES

Skerryvore, Bournemouth.
[March 7th, 1886]

Henry James,
This is what the glass says:
Where the bells peal far at sea,
Cunning fingers fashioned me.
There on palace walls I hung
While that Consuelo sung;
But I heard, though I listened well,
Never a note, never a trill,
Never a beat of the chiming bell.

Henry James,

    This is what the glass says:
Where the bells peal far at sea,
Cunning fingers fashioned me.
There on palace walls I hung
While that Consuelo sung;
But I heard, though I listened well,
Never a note, never a trill,
Never a heat of the chiming bell.
There I hung and looked; and there
In my gray face, faces fair
Shone from under shining hair
Well I saw the poising head,
But the lips moved and nothing said.
And when lights were in the hall,
Silent moved the dancers all.

So awhile I glowed; and then
Fell on dusty days and men.
Long I slumbered packed in straw.

And no one ~~but~~ the dealers saw;
Till before my silent eye
One who Sees came passing by

Now with an outlandish grace,
To the sparkling fire I pace
In the blue room at Skerryvore;
And I wait until the door
Open, and the Prince of men
Henry James, shall come again

There I hung and looked; and there
In my gray face, faces fair
Shone from under shining hair.
Well I saw the poising head,
But the lips moved and nothing said.
And when lights were in the hall,
Silent moved the dancers all.

So awhile I glowed; and then
Fell on dusty days and men.
Long I slumbered packed in straw,
And no one but the dealers saw;
Till before my silent eye
One who Sees came passing by.

Now with an outlandish grace,
To the sparkling fire I face
In the blue room at Skerryvore;
And I wait until the door
Open, and the Prince of men,
Henry James, shall come again.

[This poem, with a few verbal alterations, was included in *Underwoods* (1887) under the title *The Mirror Speaks*.]

9

STEVENSON TO JAMES

[*Skerryvore, Bournemouth, July 29th*, 1886]

MY DEAR JAMES,

This number* brightens up again like anything; and Hyacinth and the Prince are Ex-qui-site, sir, ex-quisite. I broke all bounds as I read it; I rejoice in that scene; it is, O, so humorous! and interesting as a novel —hear me!—I mean interesting as a novel never is.

Read Gosse's Raleigh: First Rate.

Yours ever
R. L. S.

10

STEVENSON TO JAMES

Skerryvore, Bournemouth, January, 1887
All the salutations!

MY DEAR JAMES,

I send you the first sheets of the new volume,† all that has yet reached me, the rest shall follow in course. I am

* Of *The Princess Casamassima*.
† *Memories and Portraits*.

really a very fair sort of a fellow all things considered, have done some work; a silly Xmas story (with some larks in it) which won't be out till I don't know when.* I am also considering a volume of verse,† much of which will be cast in my native speech, that very dark oracular medium: I suppose this is a folly, but what then? As the nurse says in Marryat, 'It was only a little one.'

My wife is peepy and dowie: two Scotch expressions with which I will leave you to wrestle unaided, as a preparation for my poetical works. She is a woman (as you know) not without art: the art of extracting the gloom of the eclipse from sunshine; and she has recently laboured in this field not without success or (as we used to say) not without a blessing. It is strange: 'we fell out my wife and I' the other night; she tackled me savagely for being a canary-bird; I replied (bleatingly) protesting that there was no use in turning life into King Lear; presently it was discovered that there were two dead combatants upon the field, each slain by an arrow of the truth, and we tenderly carried off each other's corpses. Here is a little comedy for Henry James to write! the beauty was each thought the other quite unscathed at first. But we had dealt shrewd stabs.

You say nothing of yourself, which I shall take to be good news. Archer's note has gone. He is, in truth, a very clever fellow that Archer, and I believe a good one. It is a

* *The Misadventures of John Nicholson.*
† *Underwoods.*

pleasant thing to see a man who can use a pen; he can: really says what he means, and says it with a manner; comes into print like one at his ease, not shamefaced and wrong-foot-foremost like the bulk of us. Well, here is luck, and here are the kindest recollections from the canary-bird and from King Lear, from the Tragic Woman and the Flimsy Man.

    ROBERT RAMSAY FERGUSSON STEVENSON.*

II

STEVENSON TO JAMES

[*Skerryvore, Bournemouth, February*, 1887]

MY DEAR JAMES,

My health has played me it in once more in the absurdest fashion, and the creature who now addresses you is but a stingy and white-faced *bouilli* out of the pot of fever, with the devil to pay in every corner of his economy. I suppose (to judge by your letter) I need not send you these sheets, which came during my collapse by the rush. I am on the start with three volumes, that one of tales,† a second one of essays,‡ and one of—ahem—verse. This is a great order, is it not? After that I shall have empty

---

* A reference to the two Scots poets, Allan Ramsay and Robert Fergusson.
 † *The Merry Men.*   ‡ *Memories and Portraits.*

lockers. All new work stands still; I was getting on well with *Jenkin** when this blessed malady unhorsed me, and sent me back to the dung-collecting trade of the re-publisher. I shall re-issue *Virg*[*inibus*] *Puer*[*isque*] as vol. I. of *Essays*, and the new vol. as vol. II. of ditto; to be sold, however, separately. This is but a dry maundering; however, I am quite unfit—'I am for action quite unfit Either of exercise or wit.' My father is in a variable state; many sorrows and perplexities environ the house of Stevenson; my mother shoots north at this hour on business of a distinctly rancid character; my father (under my wife's tutorage) proceeds to-morrow to Salisbury; I remain here in my bed and whistle; in no quarter of heaven is anything encouraging apparent, except that the good Colvin comes to the hotel here on a visit. This dreary view of life is somewhat blackened by the fact that my head aches, which I always regard as a liberty on the part of the powers that be. This is also my first letter since my recovery. God speed your laudatory pen!

My wife joins in all warm messages.   Yours,
R. L. S.

* *Memoir of Fleeming Jenkin* (1887).

12

STEVENSON TO JAMES*

Grand Hôtel & Bains Frascati,
Plage du Havre   August 22 [1887]

It is a fine James, & a very fine Henry James, and a remarkably fine wine; and as for the boat, it is a dam bad boat, and we are all very rough mariners. We wish you were with us, to draw our fellow fools; they are an inimitable lot: we have with us a BORE (B. Bororum) to whom your facile pen &c. All salute you: all drink to you daily—

> "The moon in the cream was dimmed by a ripple
>   affording a chequered delight.
> When the gay jolly Tars passed the word for a tipple."

Which affords a delight unchequered—
                              R. L. S.

---

* On August 21 Stevenson, his wife and stepson, his mother and a French maid, had embarked at Tilbury in the *Ludgate Hill*. They put in at Le Havre for a cargo of horses and a consignment of apes, and it may have been during an interval ashore that Stevenson collected the headed notepaper on which he thanks James for the case of champagne which he had himself taken to the ship as a parting present to the travellers.

Plage du Havre

Grand Hôtel & Bains Frascati

August 22.

It is a fine James, & a very fine Henry James, and a remarkably fine wine; and as for the boat, it is a dam bad boat, and we are all very unght mariners. We wish you were with us, to draw our fellow fools; they are an inimitable lot: we have with us a BORE (B. Bororum) to whom your facile pen &c. All salute you; all drink to you daily —

"The moon on the ocean was dimmed by a ripple
 affording a chequered delight.
 When the gay jolly Tars passed the word for the tipple"
 which affords a delight unchequered —

R. L. S.

13

STEVENSON TO JAMES

[*Newport, Long Island, U.S.A., September*, 1887]

My dear James,

Here we are at Newport, in the house of the good Fairchilds; and a sad burthen we have laid upon their shoulders. I have been in bed practically ever since I came. I caught a cold on the Banks after having had the finest time conceivable, and enjoyed myself more than I could have hoped on board our strange floating menagerie: stallions and monkeys and matches made our cargo; and the vast continent of these incongruities rolled the while like a haystack; and the stallions stood hypnotised by the motion, looking through the ports at our dinner-table, and winked when the crockery was broken; and the little monkeys stared at each other in their cages, and were thrown overboard like little bluish babies; and the big monkey, Jacko, scoured about the ship and rested willingly in my arms, to the ruin of my clothing; and the man of the stallions made a bower of the black tarpaulin, and sat therein at the feet of a raddled divinity, like a picture on a box of chocolates; and the other passengers, when they were not sick, looked on and laughed. Take all this picture, and make it roll till the bell shall sound unexpected notes and the fittings shall break loose in our state-room, and you have the voyage of the *Ludgate Hill*. She arrived in the port of New York, without beer, porter, soda-water, curaçoa, fresh meat, or fresh water; and yet we lived, and we regret her.

My wife is a good deal run down, and I am no great shakes.

America is, as I remarked, a fine place to eat in, and a great place for kindness; but, Lord, what a silly thing is popularity! I envy the cool obscurity of Skerryvore. If it even paid, said Meanness! and was abashed at himself.

Yours most sincerely,
ROBERT LOUIS STEVENSON.

14

ROBERT LOUIS STEVENSON*

BY HENRY JAMES

I

IF there be a writer of our language, at the present moment, who has the effect of making us forget the extinction of the pleasant fashion of the literary portrait, it is certainly the bright particular genius whose name is written at the head of these remarks. Mr. Stevenson fairly

* Published in the *Century Magazine*, April 1888, with a facsimile of Stevenson's signature as heading; but written in 1887 and shown to Stevenson in proof that autumn. It was later reprinted in *Partial Portraits* (1888).

challenges portraiture, as we pass him on the highway of literature (if that be the road, rather than some wandering, sun-checkered by-lane that he may be said to follow), just as the possible model, in local attire, challenges the painter who wanders through the streets of a foreign town looking for subjects. He gives us new ground to wonder why the effort to fix a face and figure, to seize a literary character and transfer it to the canvas of the critic, should have fallen into such discredit among us and have given way to the mere multiplication of little private judgment-seats, where the scales and the judicial wig, both of them considerably awry and not rendered more august by the company of a vicious-looking switch, have taken the place, as the symbols of office, of the kindly, disinterested palette and brush. It has become the fashion to be effective at the expense of the sitter, to make some little point, or inflict some little dig, with a heated party air, rather than to catch a talent in the face, follow its line, and put a finger on its essence; so that the exquisite art of criticism, smothered in grossness, finds itself turned into a question of 'sides.' The critic industriously keeps his score, but it is seldom to be hoped that the author, criminal though he may be, will be apprehended by justice through the handbills given out in the case; for it is of the essence of a happy description that it shall have been preceded by a happy observation and a free curiosity; and desuetude, as we say, has overtaken these amiable, uninvidious faculties, which have not the advantage of organs and chairs.

I hasten to add that it is not the purpose of these few pages to restore their lustre, or to bring back the more penetrating vision of which we lament the disappearance. No individual can bring it back, for the light that we look at things by is, after all, made by all of us. It is sufficient to note, in passing, that if Mr. Stevenson had presented himself in an age or in a country of portraiture, the painters would certainly each have had a turn at him. The easels and benches would have bristled, the circle would have been close, and quick, from the canvas to the sitter, the rising and falling of heads. It has happened to all of us to have gone into a studio, a studio of pupils, and seen the thick cluster of bent backs and the conscious model in the midst. It has happened to us to be struck, or not to be struck, with the beauty or the symmetry of this personage, and to have made some remark which, whether expressing admiration or disappointment, has elicited from one of the attentive workers the exclamation, 'Character—character is what he has!' These words may be applied to Mr. Robert Louis Stevenson: in the language of that art which depends most on observation, character—character is what he has. He is essentially a model, in the sense of a sitter; I do not mean, of course, in the sense of a pattern or a guiding light. And if the figures who have a life in literature may also be divided into two great classes, we may add that he is conspicuously one of the draped; he would never, if I may be allowed the expression, pose for the nude. There are writers who present themselves before the critic with just the amount of drapery that is necessary for decency, but Mr. Stevenson is not one of these; he makes his appearance in an amplitude of costume. His costume is part of the character of which I just now spoke; it never occurs to us to ask how he would look without it. Before all things he is a writer with a style—a model with a complexity of curious and picturesque garments. It is by the cut and the colour of this rich and becoming frippery—I use the term endearingly, as a painter might—that he arrests the eye and solicits the brush.

That is, frankly, half the charm he has for us, that he wears a dress and wears it with courage, with a certain cock of the hat and tinkle of the supererogatory sword; or, in other words, that he is curious of expression, and regards the literary form not simply as a code of signals, but as the keyboard of a piano and as so much plastic material. He has that vice deplored by Mr. Herbert Spencer, a manner—a manner for a manner's sake, it may sometimes doubtless be said. He is as different as possible from the sort of writer who regards words as numbers and a page as the mere addition of them; much more, to carry out our image, the dictionary stands for him as a wardrobe, and a proposition as a button for his coat. Mr. William Archer, in an article* so gracefully and ingeniously turned that the writer may almost be accused

* 'R. L. Stevenson: his Style and Thought.' *Time*, November, 1885.

of imitating even while he deprecates, speaks of him as a votary of 'lightness of touch' at any cost, and remarks that 'he is not only philosophically content, but deliberately resolved, that his readers shall look first to his manner and only in the second place to his matter.' I shall not attempt to gainsay this; I cite it rather, for the present, because it carries out my own sense. Mr. Stevenson delights in a style, and his own has nothing accidental or diffident; it is eminently conscious of its responsibilities and meets them with a kind of gallantry—as if language were a pretty woman and a person who proposes to handle it had, of necessity, to be something of a Don Juan. This element of the gallant is a noticeable part of his nature, and it is rather odd that, at the same time, a striking feature of that nature should be an absence of care for things feminine. His books are for the most part books without women, and it is not women who fall most in love with them. But Mr. Stevenson does not need, as we may say, a petticoat to inflame him; a happy collocation of words will serve the purpose, or a singular image, or the bright eye of a passing conceit, and he will carry off a pretty paradox without so much as a scuffle. The tone of letters is in him—the tone of letters as distinct from that of philosophy or of those industries whose uses are supposed to be immediate. Many readers, no doubt, consider that he carries it too far; they manifest an impatience for some glimpse of his moral message. They may be heard to ask what it is he proposes to deduce, to prove, to establish, with such a variety of paces and graces.

The main thing that he establishes, to my own perception, is that it is a delight to read him and that he renews this delight by a constant variety of experiment. Of this anon, however; and meanwhile it may be noted as a curious characteristic of current fashions that the writer whose effort is perceptibly that of the artist is very apt to find himself thrown on the defensive. A work of literature is a form, but the author who betrays a consciousness of the responsibilities involved in this circumstance not rarely perceives himself to be regarded as an uncanny personage. The usual judgment is that he may be artistic, but that he must not be too much so; that way, apparently, lies something worse than madness. This queer superstition has so successfully imposed itself that the mere fact of having been indifferent to such a danger constitutes in itself an originality. How few they are in number and how soon we could name them, the writers of English prose, at the present moment, the quality of whose prose is personal, expressive, renewed at each attempt! The state of things that would have been expected to be the rule has become the exception, and an exception for which, most of the time, an apology appears to be thought necessary. A mill that grinds with regularity and with a certain commercial fineness—that is the image suggested by the manner of a good many of the fraternity. They turn out an article for which there is a demand, they keep a shop for a speciality, and the business is carried on in accordance with a useful, well-tested prescription. It is just because he has no speciality that Mr. Stevenson is an individual, and because his curiosity is the only receipt by which he produces. Each of his books is an independent effort—a window opened to a different view. *Dr. Jekyll and Mr. Hyde* is as dissimilar as possible from *Treasure Island*; *Virginibus Puerisque* has nothing in common with *The New Arabian Nights*, and I should never have supposed *A Child's Garden of Verses* to be from the hand of the author of *Prince Otto*.

Though Mr. Stevenson cares greatly for his phrase, as every writer should who respects himself and his art, it takes no very attentive reading of his volumes to show that it is not what he cares for most, and that he regards an expressive style only, after all, as a means. It seems to me the fault of Mr. Archer's interesting paper that it suggests too much that the author of these volumes considers the art of expression as an end—a game of words. He finds that Mr. Stevenson is not serious, that he neglects a whole side of life, that he has no perception, and no consciousness, of suffering; that he speaks as a happy but heartless pagan, living only in his senses (which the critic admits to be exquisitely fine), and that, in a world full of heaviness, he is not sufficiently aware of the philosophic limitations of mere technical skill. (In sketching these aberrations Mr. Archer himself, by the way, displays anything but ponderosity of hand.) He is not the first reader, and he will not be the last, who shall have been irritated by Mr. Stevenson's jauntiness. That jauntiness is an essential part of his genius; but, to my sense, it ceases to be irritating—it indeed becomes positively touching, and constitutes an appeal to sympathy and even to tenderness—when once one has perceived what lies beneath the dancing-tune to which he mostly moves. Much as he cares for his phrase he cares more for life, and for a certain transcendently lovable part of it. He feels, as it seems to us, and that is not given to every one; this constitutes a philosophy which Mr. Archer fails to read between his lines—the respectable, desirable moral which many a reader doubtless finds that he neglects to point. He does not feel everything equally, by any manner of means; but his feelings are always his reasons; he regards them, whatever they may be, as sufficiently honourable, does not disguise them in other names or colours, and looks at whatever he meets in the brilliant candle-light that they shed. As in his extreme artistic vivacity he seems really disposed to try everything, he has tried once, by way of a change, to be inhuman, and there is a hard glitter about *Prince Otto* which seems to indicate that in this case, too, he has succeeded, as he has done in most of the feats that he has attempted. But *Prince Otto* is even less like his other productions than his other productions are like each other.

The part of life that he cares for most is youth, and the direct expression of the love of youth is the beginning and the end of his message. His appreciation of this delightful period amounts to a passion; and a passion, in the age in which we live, strikes us, on the whole, as a sufficient philosophy. It ought to satisfy Mr. Archer, and there are writers graver than Mr. Stevenson on whose behalf no such moral motive can be alleged. Mingled with his almost equal love of a literary surface it represents a real originality. This combination is the key-note of Mr. Stevenson's faculty and the explanation of his perversities. The feelings of one's teens, and even of an earlier period (for the delights of crawling, and almost of the rattle, are embodied in *A Child's Garden of Verses*), and the feeling for happy turns—these, in the last analysis (and his sense of a happy turn is of the subtlest), are the corresponding halves of his character. If *Prince Otto* and *Dr. Jekyll* left me a clearer field for the assertion, I should say that everything he has written is a direct apology for boyhood; or rather (for it must be confessed that Mr. Stevenson's tone is seldom apologetic) a direct rhapsody on the age of little jackets. Even members of the very numerous class who have held their breath over *Treasure Island* may shrug their shoulders at this account of the author's religion; but it is none the less a great pleasure—the highest reward of observation—to put one's hand on a rare illustration, and Mr. Stevenson is certainly rare. What makes him so is the singular maturity of the expression that he has given to young sentiments; he judges them, measures them, sees them from the outside, as well as entertains them. He describes credulity with all the resources of experience, and represents a crude stage with infinite ripeness. In a word, he is an artist accomplished even to sophistication, whose constant theme is the unsophisticated. Sometimes, as in *Kidnapped*, the art is so ripe that it lifts even the subject into the general air; the execution is so serious that the idea (the idea of a boy's romantic adventures) becomes a matter of universal relations. What he prizes most in the boy's ideal is the imaginative side of it, the capacity for successful make-believe. The general freshness in which this is a part of the gloss seems to him the divinest thing in life; considerably more divine, for instance, than the passion usually regarded as the supremely tender one. The idea of making believe appeals to him much more than the idea of making love. That delightful little book of rhymes, the *Child's Garden*, commemorates, from beginning to end, the picturing, personifying, dramatizing faculty of infancy, the view of life from the level of the nursery-fender. The volume is a wonder, for the extraordinary vividness with which it reproduces early impressions; a child might have written it if a child could see childhood from the outside, for it would seem that only a child is really near enough to the nursery-floor. And what is peculiar to Mr. Stevenson is that it is his own childhood he appears to delight in, and not the personal presence of little darlings. Oddly enough, there is no strong implication that he is fond of babies; he doesn't speak as a parent, or an uncle, or an educator—he speaks as a contemporary absorbed in his own game. That game is almost always a vision of dangers and triumphs; and if emotion, with him, infallibly resolves itself into memory, so memory is an evocation of throbs and thrills and suspense. He has given to the world the romance of boyhood, as others have produced that of the peerage, the police, and the medical profession.

This amounts to saying that what he is most curious of in life is heroism—personal gallantry, if need be, with a manner, or a banner—though he is also abundantly capable of enjoying it when it is artless. The delightful exploits of Jim Hawkins, in *Treasure Island*, are unaffectedly performed; but none the less 'the finest action is the better for a piece of purple,' as the author remarks in the paper on *The English Admirals*, in *Virginibus Puerisque*—a paper of which the moral is, largely, that 'we learn to desire a grand air in our heroes; and such a knowledge of the human stage as shall make them put the dots on their own i's and leave us in no suspense as to when they mean to be heroic.' The love of brave words as well as brave deeds—which is simply Mr. Stevenson's essential love of style—is recorded in this little paper with a charming, slightly sophistical ingenuity. 'They served their guns merrily, when it came to fighting, and they had the readiest ear for a bold, honourable sentiment of any class of men the world ever produced.' The author goes on to say that most men of high destinies have even high-sounding names. Alan Breck, in *Kidnapped*, is a wonderful picture of the union of courage and swagger; the little Jacobite adventurer, a figure worthy of Scott at his best, and representing the highest point that Mr. Stevenson's talent has reached, shows us that a marked taste for tawdry finery—tarnished and tattered, some of it, indeed, by ticklish occasions—is quite compatible with a perfectly high mettle. Alan Breck is, at bottom, a study of the love of glory, carried out with extreme psychological truth. When the love of glory is of an inferior order, the reputation is cultivated rather than the opportunity; but when it is a pure passion, the opportunity is cultivated for the sake of the reputation. Mr. Stevenson's kindness for adventurers extends even to the humblest of all, the mountebank and the strolling player, or even the peddler whom he declares that in his foreign travels he is habitually taken for, as we see in the whimsical apology for vagabonds which winds up *An Inland Voyage*. The hungry conjurer, the gymnast whose *maillot* is loose, have something of the glamour of the hero, inasmuch as they, too, pay with their person.

'To be even one of the outskirters of art leaves a fine stamp on a man's countenance.... That is the kind of thing that reconciles me to life; a ragged, tippling, incompetent old rogue, with the manners of a gentleman and the vanity of an artist, to keep up his self-respect!'

What reconciles Mr. Stevenson to life is the idea that in the first place it offers the widest field that we know of for odd doings, and that in the second these odd doings are the best of pegs to hang a sketch in three lines or a paradox in three pages.

As it is not odd, but extremely usual, to marry, he deprecates that course in *Virginibus Puerisque*, the collection of short essays which is most a record of his opinions —that is, largely, of his likes and dislikes. It all comes back to his sympathy with the juvenile, and that feeling about life which leads him to regard women as so many superfluous girls in a boy's game. They are almost wholly absent from his pages (the main exception is *Prince Otto*, though there is a Clara apiece in *The Rajah's Diamond* and *The Pavilion on the Links*), for they don't like ships and pistols and fights; they encumber the decks and require separate apartments; and, almost worst of all, have not the highest literary standard. Why should a person marry, when he might be swinging a cutlass or looking for a buried treasure? Why should he go to the altar when he might be polishing his prose? It is one of those curious, and, to my sense, fascinating inconsistencies that we encounter in Mr. Stevenson's mind that, though he takes such an interest in the childish life, he takes no interest in the fireside. He has an indulgent glance for it in the verses of the *Garden*, but to his view the normal child is the child who absents himself from the family-circle, in fact when he can, in imagination when he cannot, in the disguise of a buccaneer. Girls don't do this, and women are only grown-up girls, unless it be the delightful maiden, fit daughter of an imperial race, whom he commemorates in *An Inland Voyage*.

'A girl at school in France began to describe one of our regiments on parade to her French school-mates; and as she went on, she told me the recollection grew so vivid, she became so proud to be the countrywoman of such soldiers, and so sorry to be in another country, that her voice failed her, and she burst into tears. I have never forgotten that girl, and I think she very nearly deserves a statue. To call her a young lady, with all its niminy associations, would be to offer her an insult. She may rest assured of one thing, although she never should marry a heroic general, never see any great or immediate result of her life, she will not have lived in vain for her native land.'

There is something of that in Mr. Stevenson. When he begins to describe a British regiment on parade (or something of that sort) he, too, almost breaks down for emotion, which is why I have been careful to traverse the insinuation that he is primarily a chiseller of prose. If things had gone differently with him (I must permit myself this allusion to his personal situation, and I shall venture to follow it with two or three others), he might have been an historian of famous campaigns—a great painter of battle-pieces. Of course, however, in this capacity it would not have done for him to break down for emotion.

Although he remarks that marriage 'is a field of battle, and not a bed of roses,' he points out repeatedly that it is a terrible renunciation, and somehow, in strictness, incompatible even with honour—the sort of roving, trumpeting honour that appeals most to his sympathy. After that step

'there are no more by-path meadows where you may innocently linger, but the road lies long and straight and dusty to the grave.... You may think you had a conscience and believed in God; but what is a conscience to a wife? ... To marry is to domesticate the Recording Angel. Once you are married, there is nothing left for you, not even suicide, but to be good.... How, then, in such an atmosphere of compromise, to keep honour bright and abstain from base capitulations? ... The proper qualities of each sex are, indeed, eternally surprising to the other. Between the Latin and the Teuton races there are similar divergences, not to be bridged by the most liberal sympathy.... It is better to face the fact and know, when you marry, that you take into your life a creature of equal if unlike frailties; whose weak human heart beats no more tunefully than yours.'

If there is a grimness in that, it is as near as Mr. Stevenson ever comes to being grim, and we have only to turn the page to find the corrective—something delicately genial, at least, if not very much less sad:

' "The blind bow-boy" who smiles upon us from the end of terraces in old Dutch gardens laughingly hurls his bird-bolts among a fleeting generation. But for as fast as ever he shoots, the game dissolves and disappears into eternity from under his falling arrows; this one is gone ere he is struck; the other has but time to make one gesture and give one passionate cry; and they are all the things of a moment.'

That is an admission that though it is soon over, the great sentimental surrender is inevitable. And there is geniality too, still over the page (in regard to quite another matter), geniality, at least, for the profession of letters, in the declaration that there is

'one thing you can never make Philistine natures understand; one thing which yet lies on the surface, remains as unseizable to their wits as a high flight of metaphysics— namely, that the business of life is mainly carried on by the difficult art of literature, and according to a man's proficiency in that art shall be the freedom and fullness of his intercourse with other men.'

Yet it is difficult not to believe that the ideal in which our author's spirit might most gratefully have rested would have been the character of the paterfamilias, when the eye falls on such a charming piece of observation as these lines about children, in the admirable paper on *Child's Play*:

'If it were not for this perpetual imitation, we should be tempted to fancy they despised us outright, or only considered us in the light of creatures brutally strong and brutally silly, among whom they condescended to dwell in obedience, like a philosopher at a barbarous court.'

II

We know very little about a talent till we know where it grew up, and it would halt terribly at the start any account of the author of *Kidnapped* which should omit to insist promptly that he is a Scot of the Scots. Two facts, to my perception, go a great way to explain his composition, the first of which is that his boyhood was passed in the shadow of Edinburgh Castle, and the second, that he came of a family that had set up great lights on the coast. His grandfather, his uncle, were famous constructors of light-houses, and the name of the race is associated above all with the beautiful and beneficent tower of Skerryvore. We may exaggerate the way in which, in an imaginative youth, the sense of the 'story' of things would feed upon the impressions of Edinburgh—though I suspect it would be difficult really to do so. The streets are so full of history and poetry, of picture and song, of associations springing from strong passions and strange characters, that for my own part I find myself thinking of an urchin going and coming there as I used to think—wonderingly, enviously —of the small boys who figured as supernumeraries, pages, or imps in showy scenes at the theatre; the place seems the background, the complicated 'set' of a drama, and the children the mysterious little beings who are made free of the magic world. How must it not have beckoned on the imagination to pass and repass, on the way to school, under the Castle rock, conscious acutely, yet familiarly, of the gray citadel on the summit, lighted up with the tartans and bagpipes of Highland regiments! Mr. Stevenson's mind, from an early age, was furnished with the concrete Highlander, who must have had much of the effect that we nowadays call decorative. I encountered somewhere a fanciful paper of our author's* in which there is a reflection of half-holiday afternoons and, unless my own fancy plays me a trick, of lights red, in the winter dusk, in the high-placed windows of the Old Town —a delightful rhapsody on the penny sheets of figures for the puppet-shows of infancy, in life-like position, and awaiting the impatient yet careful scissors. 'If landscapes were sold,' he says in *Travels with a Donkey*, 'like the sheets of characters of my boyhood, one penny plain and twopence coloured, I should go the length of twopence every day of my life.'

Indeed, the colour of Scotland has entered into him altogether, and though, oddly enough, he has written but little about his native country, his happiest work shows, I think, that she has the best of his ability. *Kidnapped* (whose inadequate title I may deplore in passing) breathes in every line the feeling of moor and loch, and is the finest of his longer stories; and *Thrawn Janet*, a masterpiece in thirteen pages (lately republished in the volume of *The Merry Men*), is, among the shorter ones, the

---

* *A Penny Plain and Twopence Coloured*, which appeared in *The Magazine of Art*, April 1884, and was reprinted in *Memories and Portraits* (1887).

strongest in execution. The latter consists of a gruesome anecdote of the supernatural, related in the Scotch dialect; and the genuineness which this medium—at the sight of which, in general, the face of the reader grows long—wears in Mr. Stevenson's hands is a proof of how living the question of form always is to him, and what a variety of answers he has for it. It never would have occurred to us that the style of *Travels with a Donkey*, or *Virginibus Puerisque*, and the idiom of the parish of Balweary could be a conception of the same mind. If it is a good fortune for a genius to have had such a country as Scotland for its primary stuff, this is doubly the case when there has been a certain process of detachment, of extreme secularization. Mr. Stevenson has been emancipated—he is, as we may say, a Scotchman of the world. None other, I think, could have drawn with such a mixture of sympathetic and ironical observation the character of the canny young Lowlander David Balfour, a good boy but an exasperating. *Treasure Island*, *The New Arabian Nights*, *Prince Otto*, *Doctor Jekyll and Mr. Hyde*, are not very directly founded on observation; but that quality comes in with extreme fineness as soon as the subject is Scotch.

I have been wondering whether there is something more than this that our author's pages would tell us about him, or whether that particular something is in the mind of an admirer, because he happens to have had other lights upon it. It has been possible for so acute a critic as Mr. William Archer to read pure high spirits and the gospel of the young man rejoicing in his strength and his matutinal cold bath between the lines of Mr. Stevenson's prose. And it is a fact that the note of a morbid sensibility is so absent from his pages, they contain so little reference to infirmity and suffering, that we feel a trick has really been played upon us on discovering by accident the actual state of the case with the writer who has indulged in the most enthusiastic allusion to the joy of existence. We must permit ourselves another mention of his personal situation, for it adds immensely to the interest of volumes through which there draws so strong a current of life to know that they are not only the work of an invalid, but have largely been written in bed, in dreary 'health resorts,' in the intervals of sharp attacks. There is almost nothing in them to lead us to guess this; the direct evidence, indeed, is almost all contained in the limited compass of *The Silverado Squatters*. In such a case, however, it is the indirect that is the most eloquent, and I know not where to look for that, unless in the paper called *Ordered South* and its companion *Æs Triplex*, in *Virginibus Puerisque*. It is impossible to read *Ordered South* attentively without feeling that it is personal; the reflections it contains are from experience, not from fancy. The places and climates to which the invalid is carried to recover or to die are mainly beautiful, but

'In his heart of hearts he has to confess that they are not beautiful for him. . . . He is like an enthusiast leading about with him a stolid, indifferent tourist. There is some one by who is out of sympathy with the scene, and is not moved up to the measure of the occasion; and that some one is himself. . . . He seems to himself to touch things with muffled hands and to see through a veil. . . . Many a white town that sits far out on the promontory, many a comely fold of wood on the mountain-side, beckons and allures his imagination day after day, and is yet as inaccessible to his feet as the clefts and gorges of the clouds. The sense of distance grows upon him wonderfully; and after some feverish efforts and the fretful uneasiness of the first few days he falls contentedly in with the restrictions of his weakness. . . . He feels, if he is to be thus tenderly weaned from the passion of life, thus gradually inducted into the slumber of death, that when at last the end comes it will come quietly and fitly. . . . He will pray for Medea: when she comes, let her rejuvenate or slay.'

The second of the short essays I have mentioned has a taste of mortality only because the purpose of it is to insist that the only sane behaviour is to leave death and the accidents that lead to it out of our calculations. Life 'is a honeymoon with us all through, and none of the longest. Small blame to us if we give our whole hearts to this glowing bride of ours'; the person who does so 'makes a very different acquaintance with the world, keeps all his pulses going true and fast, and gathers impetus as he runs, until, if he be running towards anything better than wildfire, he may shoot up and become a constellation in the end.' Nothing can be more deplorable than to 'forgo all the issues of living in a parlour with a regulated temperature.' Mr. Stevenson adds that as for those whom the gods love dying young, a man dies too young at whatever age he parts with life. The testimony of *Æs Triplex* to the author's own disabilities is, after all, very indirect; it consists mainly in the general protest not so much against the fact of extinction as against the theory of it. The reader only asks himself why the hero of *Travels with a Donkey*, the historian of Alan Breck, should think of these things. His appreciation of the active side of life has such a note of its own that we are surprised to find that it proceeds in a considerable measure from an intimate acquaintance with the passive. It seems too anomalous that the writer who has most cherished the idea of a certain free exposure should also be the one who has been reduced most to looking for it within, and that the figures of adventurers who, at least in our literature of to-day, are the most vivid, should be the most vicarious. The truth is, of course, that, as the *Travels with a Donkey* and *An Inland Voyage* abundantly show, the author has a fund of reminiscences. He did not spend his younger years 'in a parlour with a regulated temperature.' A reader who happens to be aware of how much it has been his later fate to do so may be excused for finding an added source of interest—something, indeed, deeply and constantly touching—in this association of peculiarly restrictive conditions with the vision of high spirits and romantic accidents of a kind of honourably picturesque career.

Mr. Stevenson is, however, distinctly, in spite of his occasional practice of the gruesome, a frank optimist, an observer who not only loves life, but does not shrink from the responsibility of recommending it. There is a systematic brightness in him which testifies to this and which is, after all, but one of the innumerable ingenuities of patience. What is remarkable in his case is that his productions should constitute an exquisite expression, a sort of whimsical gospel, of enjoyment. The only difference between *An Inland Voyage*, or *Travels with a Donkey* and *The New Arabian Nights*, or *Treasure Island*, or *Kidnapped*, is, that in the later books the enjoyment is reflective,—though it simulates spontaneity with singular art, —whereas in the first two it is natural and, as it were, historical.

These little histories—the first volumes, if I mistake not, that introduced Mr. Stevenson to lovers of good writing—abound in charming illustrations of his disposition to look at the world as a not exactly refined, but glorified, pacified Bohemia. They narrate the quest of personal adventure—on one occasion in a canoe on the Sambre and the Oise, and on another at a donkey's tail over the hills and valleys of the Cévennes. I well remember that when I read them, in their novelty, upward of ten years ago, I seemed to see the author, unknown as yet to fame, jump before my eyes into a style. His steps in literature presumably had not been many; yet he had mastered his form—it had in these cases, perhaps, more substance than his matter—and a singular air of literary experience. It partly, though not completely, explains the phenomenon, that he had already been able to write the exquisite little story of *Will of the Mill*, published previously to *An Inland Voyage*, and now republished in the volume of *The Merry Men*; for in *Will of the Mill* there is something exceedingly rare, poetical, and unexpected, with that most fascinating quality a work of imagination can have, a dash of alternative mystery as to its meaning, an air—the air of life itself—of half inviting, half defying, you to interpret. This brief but finished composition stood in the same relation to the usual 'magazine story' that a glass of Johannisberg occupies to a draught of table d'hôte *vin ordinaire*.

'One evening, he asked the miller where the river went. . . . "It goes out into the lowlands, and waters the great corn country, and runs through a sight of fine cities (so they say) where kings live all alone in great palaces, with a sentry walking up and down before the door. And it goes under bridges with stone men upon them, looking down and smiling so curious at the water, and living folks leaning their elbows on the wall and looking over too. And then it goes on and on, and down through marshes and sands, until at last it falls into the sea, where the ships are that bring parrots and tobacco from the Indies."'

It is impossible not to open one's eyes at such a paragraph as that, especially if one has taken a common texture for granted. Will of the Mill spends his life in the valley through which the river runs, and through which, year after year, post-chaises and wagons, and pedestrians, and once an army, 'horse and foot, cannon and tumbrel, drum and standard,' take their way, in spite of the dreams he has once had of seeing the mysterious world, and it is not till death comes that he goes on his travels. He ends by keeping an inn, where he converses with many more initiated spirits, and though he is an amiable man, he dies a bachelor, having broken off, with more plainness than he would have used had he been less untravelled—of course he remains sadly provincial—his engagement to the parson's daughter. The story is in the happiest key, and suggests all kinds of things, but what does it in particular represent? The advantage of waiting, perhaps—the valuable truth, that, one by one, we tide over our impatiences. There are sagacious people who hold that if one doesn't answer a letter it ends by answering itself. So the sub-title of Mr. Stevenson's tale might be 'The Beauty of Procrastination.' If you don't indulge your curiosities your slackness itself makes at last a kind of rich element, and it comes to very much the same thing in the end. When it came to the point, poor Will had not even the curiosity to marry; and the author leaves us in stimulating doubt as to whether he judges him too selfish or only too philosophic.

I find myself speaking of Mr. Stevenson's last volume (at the moment I write) before I have spoken, in any detail, of its predecessors, which I must let pass as a sign that I lack space for a full enumeration. I may mention two more of his productions as completing the list of those that have a personal reference. *The Silverado Squatters* describes a picnicking episode, undertaken on grounds of health, on a mountain-top in California; but this free sketch, which contains a hundred humorous touches, and in the figure of Irvine Lovelands one of Mr. Stevenson's most veracious portraits, is perhaps less vivid, as it is certainly less painful, than those other pages in which, some years ago, he commemorated the twelvemonth he spent in America—the history of a journey from New York to San Francisco in an emigrant-train, performed as the sequel to a voyage across the Atlantic in the same severe conditions.* He has never made his points better than in that half-humorous, half-tragical recital, nor given a more striking instance of his talent for reproducing the feeling of queer situations and contacts. It is much to be regretted that this little masterpiece has not been brought to light a second time, as also that he has not given the world—as I believe he came very near doing— his observations in the steerage of an Atlantic liner.† If, as I say, our author has a taste for the impressions

* *Across the Plains* (*Longman's Magazine*, July–August, 1883) was published in book form in 1892.

† *The Amateur Emigrant*; Stevenson wrote it when hard pressed for money in California in 1879, and had a poor opinion of it. On his return to Scotland his father bought back the rights and it was not published until 1895.

of Bohemia, he has been very consistent and has not shrunk from going far afield in search of them. And as I have already been indiscreet, I may add that if it has been his fate to be converted in fact from the sardonic view of matrimony, this occurred under an influence which should have the particular sympathy of American readers. He went to California for his wife; and Mrs. Stevenson, as appears moreover by the title-page of the work, has had a hand—evidently a light and practised one—in *The Dynamiter*, the second series, characterized by a rich extravagance, of *The New Arabian Nights*. *The Silverado Squatters* is the history of a honeymoon—prosperous, it would seem, putting Irvine Lovelands aside, save for the death of dog Chuchu 'in his teens, after a life so shadowed and troubled, continually shaken with alarms, and the tear of elegant sentiment permanently in his eye.'

Mr. Stevenson has a theory of composition in regard to the novel, on which he is to be congratulated, as any positive and genuine conviction of this kind is vivifying so long as it is not narrow. The breath of the novelist's being is his liberty; and the incomparable virtue of the form he uses is that it lends itself to views innumerable and diverse, to every variety of illustration. There is certainly no other mould of so large a capacity. The doctrine of M. Zola himself, so meagre if literally taken, is fruitful, inasmuch as in practice he romantically departs from it. Mr. Stevenson does not need to depart, his individual taste being as much to pursue the romantic as his principle is to defend it. Fortunately, in England to-day, it is not much attacked. The triumphs that are to be won in the portrayal of the strange, the improbable, the heroic, especially as these things shine from afar in the credulous eye of youth, are his strongest, most constant incentive. On one happy occasion, in relating the history of *Doctor Jekyll*, he has seen them as they present themselves to a maturer vision. *Doctor Jekyll* is not a 'boys' book,' nor yet is *Prince Otto*; the latter, however, is not, like the former, an experiment in mystification—it is, I think, more than anything else, an experiment in style, conceived one summer's day, when the author had given the reins to his high appreciation of Mr. George Meredith. It is perhaps the most literary of his works, but it is not the most natural. It is one of those coquetries, as we may call them for want of a better word, which may be observed in Mr. Stevenson's activity—a kind of artful inconsequence. It is easy to believe that if his strength permitted him to be a more abundant writer he would still more frequently play this eminently literary trick—that of dodging off in a new direction—upon those who might have fancied they knew all about him. I made the reflection, in speaking of *Will of the Mill*, that there is a kind of anticipatory malice in the subject of that fine story; as if the writer had intended to say to his reader, 'You will never guess, from the unction with which I describe the life of a man who never stirred five miles from home, that I am destined to make my greatest hits in treating of the rovers of the deep.' Even here, however, the author's characteristic irony would have come in; for—the rare chances of life being what he most keeps his eye on—the uncommon belongs as much to the way the inquiring Will sticks to his door-sill as to the incident, say, of John Silver and his men, when they are dragging Jim Hawkins to his doom, hearing, in the still woods of Treasure Island, the strange hoot of the Maroon.

The novelist who leaves the extraordinary out of his account is liable to awkward confrontations, as we are compelled to reflect in this age of newspapers and of universal publicity. The next report of the next divorce case—to give an instance—shall offer us a picture of astounding combinations of circumstance and behaviour, and the annals of any energetic race are rich in curious anecdote and startling example. That interesting compilation, *Vicissitudes of Families,* is but a superficial record of strange accidents; the family—taken, of course, in the long piece—is, as a general thing, a catalogue of odd specimens and strong situations, and we must remember that the most singular products are those which are not exhibited. Mr. Stevenson leaves so wide a margin for the wonderful—it impinges with easy assurance upon the text—that he escapes the danger of being brought up by cases he has not allowed for. When he allows for Mr. Hyde he allows for everything; and one feels, moreover, that even if he did not wave so gallantly the flag of the imaginary and contend that the improbable is what has most character, he would still insist that we ought to make believe. He would say we ought to make believe that the extraordinary is the best part of life, even if it were not, and to do so because the finest feelings—suspense, daring, decision, passion, curiosity, gallantry, eloquence, friendship—are involved in it, and it is of infinite importance that the tradition of these precious things should not perish. He would prefer, in a word, any day in the week, Alexandre Dumas to Honoré de Balzac; and it is, indeed, my impression that he prefers the author of *The Three Musketeers* to any novelist except Mr. George Meredith. I should go so far as to suspect that his ideal of the delightful work of fiction would be the adventures of Monte Cristo related by the author of *Richard Feverel*. There is some magnanimity in his esteem for Alexandre Dumas, inasmuch as in *Kidnapped* he has put into a fable worthy of that inventor a fineness of grain with which Dumas never had anything to do. He makes us say, Let the tradition live, by all means, since it was delightful; but at the same time he is the cause of our perceiving afresh that a tradition is kept alive only by something being added to it. In this particular case—in *Doctor Jekyll* and *Kidnapped*—Mr. Stevenson has added psychology.

The New Arabian Nights offers us, as the title indicates, the wonderful in the frankest, most delectable form. Partly extravagant, and partly very specious, they are the result of a very happy idea, that of placing a series of adventures which are pure adventures in the setting of contemporary English life, and relating them in the placidly ingenious tone of Scheherezade. This device is carried to perfection in *The Dynamiter*, where the manner takes on more of a kind of high-flown serenity in proportion as the incidents are more 'steep.' In this line *The Suicide Club* is Mr. Stevenson's greatest success; and the first two pages of it, not to mention others, live in the memory. For reasons which I am conscious of not being able to represent as sufficient, I find something ineffaceably impressive—something really haunting—in the incident of Prince Florizel and Colonel Geraldine, who, one evening in March, are 'driven by a sharp fall of sleet into an Oyster Bar in the immediate neighbourhood of Leicester Square,' and there have occasion to observe the entrance of a young man followed by a couple of commissionaires, each of whom carries a large dish of creamtarts under a cover—a young man who 'pressed these confections on every one's acceptance with exaggerated courtesy.' There is no effort at a picture here, but the imagination makes one of the lighted interior, the London sleet outside, the company that we guess, given the locality, and the strange politeness of the young man, leading on to circumstances stranger still. This is what may be called putting one in the mood for a story. But Mr. Stevenson's most brilliant stroke of that kind is the opening episode of *Treasure Island*—the arrival of the brown old seaman, with a sabre cut, at the 'Admiral Benbow,' and the advent, not long after, of the blind sailor, with a green shade over his eyes, who comes tapping down the road, in quest of him, with his stick. *Treasure Island* is a 'boy's book,' in the sense that it embodies a boy's vision of the extraordinary; but it is unique in this, and calculated to fascinate the weary mind of experience, that what we see in it is not only the ideal fable, but, as part and parcel of that, as it were, the young reader himself and his state of mind: we seem to read it over his shoulder, with an arm around his neck. It is all as perfect as a well-played boy's game, and nothing can exceed the spirit and skill, the humour and the open air feeling, with which the whole thing is kept at the critical pitch. It is not only a record of queer chances, but a study of young feelings; there is a moral side in it, and the figures are not puppets with vague faces. If Jim Hawkins illustrates successful daring, he does so with a delightful, rosy good-boyishness, and a conscious, modest liability to error. His luck is tremendous, but it doesn't make him proud; and his manner is refreshingly provincial and human. So is that, even more, of the admirable John Silver, one of the most picturesque, and, indeed, in every way, most genially presented, villains in the whole literature of romance. He has a singularly distinct and expressive countenance, which, of course, turns out to be a grimacing mask. Never was a mask more knowingly, vividly painted. *Treasure Island* will surely become—it must already have become, and will remain—in its way a classic; thanks to this indescribable mixture of the prodigious and the human, of surprising coincidences and familiar feelings. The language in which Mr. Stevenson has chosen to tell his story is an admirable vehicle for these feelings; with its humorous braveries and quaintnesses, its echoes of old ballads and yarns, it touches all kinds of sympathetic chords.

Is *Dr. Jekyll and Mr. Hyde* a work of high philosophic intention, or simply the most ingenious and irresponsible of fictions? It has the stamp of a really imaginative production, that we may take it in different ways, but I suppose it would be called the most serious of the author's tales. It deals with the relation of the baser parts of man to his nobler—of the capacity for evil that exists in the most generous natures, and it expresses these things in a fable which is a wonderfully happy invention. The subject is endlessly interesting, and rich in all sorts of provocation, and Mr. Stevenson is to be congratulated on having touched the core of it. I may do him injustice, but it is, however, here, not the profundity of the idea which strikes me so much as the art of the presentation—the extremely successful form. There is a genuine feeling for the perpetual moral question, a fresh sense of the difficulty of being good and the brutishness of being bad, but what there is above all is a singular ability in holding the interest. I confess that that, to my sense, is the most edifying thing in the short, rapid, concentrated story, which is really a masterpiece of concision. There is something almost impertinent in the way, as I have noticed, in which

Mr. Stevenson achieves his best effects without the aid of the ladies, and *Dr. Jekyll* is a capital example of his heartless independence. It is usually supposed that a truly poignant impression cannot be made without them, but in the drama of Mr. Hyde's fatal ascendency they remain altogether in the wing. It is very obvious—I do not say it cynically—that they must have played an important part in his development. The gruesome tone of the tale is, no doubt, deepened by their absence; it is like the late afternoon light of a foggy winter Sunday, when even inanimate objects have a kind of wicked look. I remember few situations in the pages of mystifying fiction more to the purpose than the episode of Mr. Utterson's going to Dr. Jekyll's to confer with the butler, when the doctor is locked up in his laboratory and the old servant, whose sagacity has hitherto encountered successfully the problems of the sideboard and the pantry, confesses that this time he is utterly baffled. The way the two men, at the door of the laboratory, discuss the identity of the mysterious personage inside, who has revealed himself in two or three inhuman glimpses to Poole, has those touches of which irresistible shudders are made. The butler's theory is that his master has been murdered, and that the murderer is in the room, personating him with a sort of clumsy diabolism. 'Well, when that masked thing like a monkey jumped from among the chemicals and whipped into the cabinet, it went down my spine like ice.' That is the effect upon the reader of most of the story. I say of most rather than all, because the ice rather melts in the sequel, and I have some difficulty in accepting the business of the powders, which seems to me too explicit and explanatory. The powders constitute the machinery of the transformation, and it will probably have struck many readers that this uncanny process would be more conceivable (so far as one may speak of the conceivable in such a case), if the author had not made it so definite.

I have left Mr. Stevenson's best book to the last, as it is also the last he has given, at the present speaking, to the public—the tales comprising *The Merry Men* having already appeared; but I find that, on the way, I have anticipated some of the remarks that I had intended to make about it. That which is most to the point is that there are parts of it so fine as to suggest that the author's talent has taken a fresh start, various as have been the impulses in which it had already indulged, and serious the impediments among which it is condemned to exert itself. There would have been a kind of perverse humility in his keeping up the fiction that a production so literary as *Kidnapped* is addressed to immature minds; and though it was originally given to the world, I believe, in a 'boy's paper,' the story embraces every occasion that it meets to satisfy the higher criticism. It has two weak spots, which need simply to be mentioned. The cruel and miserly uncle, in the first chapters, is rather in the tone of superseded tradition, and the tricks he plays upon his ingenuous nephew are a little like those of country conjurors;

in these pages we feel that Mr. Stevenson is thinking too much of what a 'boy's paper' is expected to contain. Then the history stops without ending, as it were; but I think I may add that this accident speaks for itself. Mr. Stevenson has often to lay down his pen for reasons that have nothing to do with the failure of inspiration, and the last page of David Balfour's adventures is an honourable plea for indulgence. The remaining five-sixths of the book deserve to stand by *Henry Esmond*, as a fictive autobiography in archaic form. The author's sense of the English idiom of the last century, and still more of the Scotch, have enabled him to give a gallant companion to Thackeray's *tour de force*. The life, the humour, the colour of the central portions of *Kidnapped* have a singular pictorial virtue; these passages read like a series of inspired footnotes on some historic page. The charm of the most romantic episode in the world—though perhaps it would be hard to say why it is the most romantic, when it was intermingled with so much stupidity—is over the whole business, and the forlorn hope of the Stuarts is revived for us without evoking satiety. There could be no better instance of the author's talent for seeing the actual in the marvellous, and reducing the extravagant to plausible detail, than the description of Alan Breck's defence in the cabin of the ship, and the really magnificent chapters of 'The Flight in the Heather.' Mr. Stevenson has, in a high degree (and doubtless for good reasons of his own), what may be called the imagination of physical states, and this has enabled him to arrive at a wonderfully exact notation of the miseries of his panting Lowland hero, dragged for days and nights over hill and dale, through bog and thicket, without meat or drink or rest, at the tail of an Homeric Highlander. The great superiority of the book resides, to my mind, however, in the fact that it puts two characters on their feet in an admirably upright way. I have paid my tribute to Alan Breck, and I can only repeat that he is a masterpiece. It is interesting to observe that, though the man is extravagant, the author's touch exaggerates nothing; it is, throughout, of the most truthful, genial, ironical kind, full of penetration, but with none of the grossness of moralizing satire. The figure is a genuine study, and nothing can be more charming than the way Mr. Stevenson both sees through it and admires it. Shall I say that he sees through David Balfour? This would be, perhaps, to underestimate the density of that medium. Beautiful, at any rate, is the expression which this unfortunate though circumspect youth gives to those qualities which combine to excite our respect and our objurgations in the Scottish character. Such a scene as the episode of the quarrel of the two men on the mountain-side is a real stroke of genius, and has the very logic and rhythm of life —a quarrel which we feel to be inevitable, though it is about nothing, or almost nothing, and which springs from exasperated nerves and the simple shock of temperaments. The author's vision of it has a profundity which goes deeper, I think, than *Dr. Jekyll*. I know of few better examples of the way genius has ever a surprise in its pockets—keeps an ace, as it were, up its sleeve. And in this case it endears itself to us by making us reflect that such a passage as the one I speak of is in fact a signal proof of what the novel can do at its best and what nothing else can do so well. In the presence of this sort of success we perceive its immense value. It is capable of a rare transparency—it can illustrate human affairs in cases so delicate and complicated that any other vehicle would be clumsy. To those who love the art that Mr. Stevenson practises he will appear, in pointing this incidental moral, not only to have won a particular triumph, but to have given a delightful pledge.

15

STEVENSON TO JAMES

[*Saranac Lake, Adirondacks, N.Y., October,* 1887]
I know not the day; but the month it is the drear October by the ghoul-haunted woodland of Weir.

MY DEAR HENRY JAMES,

This is to say *First*, the voyage was a huge success. We all enjoyed it (bar my wife) to the ground: sixteen days at sea with a cargo of hay, matches, stallions, and monkeys, and in a ship with no style on, and plenty of sailors to talk to, and the endless pleasures of the sea—

the romance of it, the sport of the scratch dinner and the smashing of crockery, the pleasure—an endless pleasure—of balancing to the swell: well, it's over.

Second, I had a fine time, rather a troubled one, at Newport and New York; saw much of and liked hugely the Fairchilds, St. Gaudens the sculptor, Gilder of the *Century*—just saw the dear Alexander—saw a lot of my old and admirable friend Will Low, whom I wish you knew and appreciated—was medallioned by St. Gaudens, and at last escaped to——

Third, Saranac Lake, where we now are, and which I believe we mean to like and pass the winter at. Our house—emphatically 'Baker's'—is on a hill, and has a sight of a stream turning a corner in the valley—bless the face of running water!—and sees some hills too, and the paganly prosaic roofs of Saranac itself; the Lake it does not see, nor do I regret that; I like water (fresh water I mean) either running swiftly among stones, or else largely qualified with whisky. As I write, the sun (which has been long a stranger) shines in at my shoulder; from the next room, the bell of Lloyd's typewriter makes an agreeable music as it patters off (at a rate which astonishes this experienced novelist) the early chapters of a humorous romance;* from still further off—the walls of Baker's are neither ancient nor massive—rumours of Valentine about the kitchen stove come to my ears; of my mother and Fanny I hear nothing, for the excellent reason that they have gone

* *The Wrong Box.*

sparking off, one to Niagara, one to Indianapolis. People complain that I never give news in my letters. I have wiped out that reproach.

But now, *Fourth*, I have seen the article; and it may be from natural partiality, I think it the best you have written. O—I remember the Gautier, which was an excellent performance; and the Balzac, which was good; and the Daudet, over which I licked my chops; but the R. L. S. is better yet. It is so humorous, and it hits my little frailties with so neat (and so friendly) a touch; and Alan is the occasion for so much happy talk, and the quarrel is so generously praised. I read it twice, though it was only some hours in my possession; and Low, who got it for me from the *Century*, sat up to finish it ere he returned it; and, sir, we were all delighted. Here is the paper out, nor will anything, not even friendship, not even gratitude for the article, induce me to begin a second sheet; so here, with the kindest remembrances and the warmest good wishes, I remain, yours affectionately,

R. L. S.

16

JAMES TO STEVENSON

34 De Vere Gardens, W.
October 30th, 1887

MY DEAR LOUIS,

It is really a delight to get your charming letter (from the undecipherable lake) just this very blessed minute. Long alienation has made my American geography vague, and not knowing *what* your lake is I know still less *where* it is. Nevertheless I roughly suspect it of being in the Adirondacks; if it isn't, may it excuse the injury. Let me tell you, quickly and crudely, that I am quite exhilarated that you like the Article. I thought—or rather I hoped—that you would, and yet I feared you wouldn't—*i.e.* mightn't—and altogether I was not so convinced but that your expression of pleasure is a reassurance to me as well as a gratification. I felt, while I wrote, that you served me well; you were really, my dear fellow, a capital subject—I will modestly grant you that, though it takes the bloom from my merit. To be not only witty one's self but the cause in others of a wit that is not at one's expense —that is a rare and high character, and altogether yours. I devoutly hope that it's in the November *Century* that the thing appears, and also that it was not too apparent to you in it that I hadn't seen a proof—a privation I detest. I wrote to you some three weeks or so ago—c/o

Scribner's. Wondrous seems to me the fate that leads you to the prospect of wintering at—well, wherever you are. The succession of incidents and places in your career is ever romantic. May you find what you need—white, sunny winter hours, not too stove-heated nor too pork-fed, with a crisp dry air and a frequent leisure and no desperation of inanition. And may much good prose flow from it all. I wish I could see you—in my mind's eye: but que dis-je? I do—and the minutest particularities of your wooden bower rise before me. I see the clap-boards and the piazza and the door-step and the door-handle, and the road in front and the yard behind. Don't yearn to extinction for the trim little personality of Skerryvore. I have great satisfaction in hearing (from Mrs. Procter, of course) that that sweet house is let—to those Canadians. May they be punctual with their rent. Do tell your wife, on her return from the wild West, that I *supplicate* her to write to me, with items, details, specifications, and insistences. I am now collecting some papers into a volume; and the Article, par excellence, in the midst. May the American air rest lightly on you, my dear friend: I wish it were mine to turn it on!

Ever faithfully yours,
HENRY JAMES.

P.S. My love to your wife goes without saying—but I send a very explicit friendliness to your mother. I hope she returns the liking of America. And I bless the ticking Lloyd.

17

STEVENSON TO JAMES

[*Saranac Lake, Adirondacks, N.Y., November* 1887]

MY DEAR HENRY JAMES,

It may please you to know how our family has been employed. In the silence of the snow, the afternoon lamp has lighted an eager fireside group: my mother reading, Fanny, Lloyd and I devoted listeners; and the work was really one of the best works I ever heard; and its author is to be praised and honoured; and what do you suppose is the name of it? and have you ever read it yourself? and (I am bound I will get to the bottom of the page before I blow the gaff, if I have to fight it out on this line all summer; for if you have not to turn a leaf, there can be no suspense, the conspectory eye being swift to pick out proper names; and without suspense, there can be little pleasure in this world, to my mind at least) and in short the name of it is *Roderick Hudson*, if you please. My dear James, it is very spirited, and very sound, and very noble too. Hudson, Mrs. Hudson, Rowland. O, all first rate. Rowland a very fine fellow, Hudson as good as he can stick (did you know Hudson? I suspect you did) Mrs. H. his real born mother, a thing rarely managed in fiction.

We are all keeping pretty fit and pretty hearty; but this letter is not from me to you, it is from a reader of *R. H.*

to the author of the same, and it says nothing, and has nothing to say, but Thank You.

We are going to reread *Casamassima* as a proper pendant. Sir, I think these two are your best; and care not who knows it.

May I beg you, the next time *Roderick* is printed off, to go over the sheets of the last few chapters, and strike out "immense" and "tremendous"? You have simply dropped them there like your pocket-handkerchief; all you have to do is to pick them up and pouch them, and your room—what do I say?—your cathedral!—will be swept and garnished.

I am, dear Sir,
your delighted reader
ROBERT LOUIS STEVENSON

P.S. Perhaps it is a pang of causeless honesty, perhaps I hope it will set a value on my praise of *Roderick*, perhaps it's a burst of the diabolic, but I must break out with the news that I can't bear *The Portrait of a Lady*. I read it all, and I wept too; but I can't stand your having written it; and I beg you will write no more of the like. Infra, sir: Below you: I can't help it—it may be your favourite work, but in my eyes it's BELOW YOU to write and me to read. I thought *Roderick* was going to be another such at the beginning; and I cannot describe my pleasure as I found it taking bones and blood, and looking out at me with a moved and human countenance, whose lineaments are written in my memory until my last of days.

R. L. S.

My wife begs your forgiveness: I believe for her silence.

18

JAMES TO STEVENSON

34 De Vere Gardens, W.
December 5th [1887]

MY DEAR LOUIS,

I could almost hate poor Roderick H. (in whom, at best, as <u>in all my past and shuffled off emanations and efforts, my interest is of the slenderest</u>,) for making you write so much more about him than about a still more fascinating hero. If you had only given me a small instalment of that romantic serial, The Mundane Situation of R. L. S.! My dear fellow, you skip whole numbers at a time. Your correspondent wouldn't. I am really delighted you can find something at this late day in that work in which my diminutive muse first tried to elongate her little legs. It is a book of considerable good faith, but I think of limited skill. Besides, directly my productions are finished, or at least thrust out to earn their living, they seem to *me* dead. They dwindle when weaned—removed from the parental breast, and only flourish, a little, while imbibing the milk of my plastic care. None the less am I touched by your excellent and friendly words. Perhaps I am touched even more by those you dedicate to the less favoured *Portrait*. My dear Louis, I don't think I follow you here—why does that work move you to such scorn—since you can put up with *Roderick*, or with any of the others? As they are, so it is, and as it is, so they are. Upon my word you are unfair to it—and I scratch my head bewildered. 'Tis surely a graceful, ingenious, elaborate work—with too many pages, but with (I think) an interesting subject, and a good deal of life and style. There! *All* my works may be damnable—but I don't perceive the particular damnability of that one. However I feel as if it were almost gross to defend myself—for even your censure pleases and your restrictions refresh. I have this very day received from Mr. Bain your *Memories and Portraits*, and I lick my chops in advance. It is very delectable, I can see, and it has the prettiest coat and face of any of your volumes.—London is settling to its winter pace, and the cool rich fogs curtain us in. I see Colvin once in a while *dans le monde*, which however I frequent less and less. I miss you too sensibly. My love to your wife and mother—my greeting to the brave Lloyd.

Ever yours very faithfully,
H. JAMES.

P.S. I am unspeakably vexed at the *Century's* long delay in printing my paper on you—it is quite sickening. But I am helpless—and they tell me it won't come out till *March*— d—n 'em all. I am also sorry—very—not to have any other prose specimens of my own genius to send you. I have really written a good deal lately—but the beastly periodicals hold them back: I can't make out why. But I trust the dance will begin before long, and that then you may glean some pleasure. I pray you, do write something yourself for one who *knows* and yet is famished: for there isn't a morsel here that will keep one alive. I won't question you—'twere vain—but I wish I knew more about you. I want to *see* you—where you live and *how*— and the complexion of your days. But I don't know even the name of your habitat nor the date of your letter: neither were on the page. I bless you all the same.

19

STEVENSON TO JAMES

[*Saranac Lake, March*, 1888]

MY DEAR DELIGHTFUL JAMES,

To quote your heading to my wife, I think no man writes so elegant a letter, I am sure none so kind, unless it be Colvin, and there is more of the stern parent about him. I was vexed at your account of my admired Meredith: I wish I could go and see him; as it is I will try to write; and yet (do you understand me?) there is something in that potent, *genialisch* affectation that puts one on the strain even to address him in a letter. He is not an easy man to be yourself with; there is so much of him, and the veracity and the high athletic intellectual humbug are so intermixed. I read with indescribable admiration your *Emerson*. I begin to long for the day when these portraits of yours shall be collected: do put me in. But Emerson is a higher flight. Have you a *Tourgueneff*? You have told me many interesting things of him, and I seem to see them written, and forming a graceful and *bildend* sketch. (I wonder whence comes this flood of German—I haven't opened a German book since I teethed.) My novel* is a tragedy; four parts out of six or seven are written, and gone to Burlingame. Five parts of it are sound, human tragedy; the last one or two, I regret to say, not so soundly designed; I almost hesitate to write them; they are very picturesque, but they are fantastic; they shame, perhaps degrade, the beginning. I wish I knew; that was how the tale came to me however. I got the situation; it was an old taste of mine: The older brother goes out in the '45, the younger stays; the younger, of course, gets title and estate and marries the bride designate of the elder—a family match, but he (the younger) had always loved her, and she had really loved the elder. Do you see the situation? Then the devil and Saranac suggested this *dénouement*, and I joined the two

* *The Master of Ballantrae.*

ends in a day or two of constant feverish thought, and began to write. And now—I wonder if I have not gone too far with the fantastic? The elder brother is an INCUBUS: supposed to be killed at Culloden, he turns up again and bleeds the family of money; on that stopping he comes and lives with them, whence flows the real tragedy, the nocturnal duel of the brothers (very naturally, and indeed, I think, inevitably arising), and second supposed death of the elder. Husband and wife now really make up, and then the cloven hoof appears. For the third supposed death and the manner of the third reappearance is steep; steep, sir. It is even very steep, and I fear it shames the honest stuff so far; but then it is highly pictorial, and it leads up to the death of the elder brother at the hands of the younger in a perfectly cold-blooded murder, of which I wish (and mean) the reader to approve. You see how daring is the design. There are really but six characters, and one of these episodic, and yet it covers eighteen years, and will be, I imagine, the longest of my works.

Yours ever
R. L. S.

20

STEVENSON TO JAMES

Manasquan (ahem!), New Jersey, May 28th, 1888

MY DEAR JAMES,

With what a torrent it has come at last! Up to now, what I like best is the first number of *A London Life*. You have never done anything better, and I don't know if perhaps you have ever done anything so good as the girl's outburst: tip-top. I have been preaching your later works in your native land. I had to present the *Beltraffio* volume to Low, and it has brought him to his knees; he was *amazed* at the first part of *Georgina's Reasons*, although (like me) not so well satisfied with Part II. It is annoying to find the American public as stupid as the English, but they will waken up in time: I wonder what they will think of *Two Nations?** . . .

This, dear James, is a valedictory. On June 15th the schooner yacht *Casco* will (weather and a jealous providence permitting) steam through the Golden Gates for Honolulu, Tahiti, the Galapagos, Guayaquil, and—I hope *not* the bottom of the Pacific. It will contain your obedient 'umble servant and party. It seems too good to be true, and is a very good way of getting through the

* James's story *Two Countries* appeared in *Harper's Magazine*, June 1888. When he reprinted it in *The Aspern Papers* (1888) he changed the title to *The Modern Warning*.

green-sickness of maturity which, with all its accompanying ills, is now declaring itself in my mind and life. They tell me it is not so severe as that of youth: if I (and the *Casco*) are spared, I shall tell you more exactly, as I am one of the few people in the world who do not forget their own lives.

Good-bye, then, my dear fellow, and please write us a word; we expect to have three mails in the next two months: Honolulu, Tahiti, and Guayaquil. But letters will be forwarded from Scribner's, if you hear nothing more definite directly. In 3 (three) days I leave for San Francisco. Ever yours most cordially,

R. L. S.

21

JAMES TO STEVENSON

34 De Vere Gardens, W.
July 31st [1888]

MY DEAR LOUIS,

You are too far away—you are too absent—too invisible, inaudible, inconceivable. Life is too short a business and friendship too delicate a matter for such tricks—for cutting great gory masses out of 'em by the year at a time. Therefore come back. Hang it all—sink it all and come back. A little more and I shall cease to believe in you: I don't mean (in the usual implied phrase) in your veracity, but literally and more fatally in your relevancy—your objective reality. You have become a beautiful myth—a kind of unnatural uncomfortable unburied *mort*. You put forth a beautiful monthly voice, with such happy notes in it—but it comes from too far away, from the other side of the globe, while I vaguely know that you are crawling like a fly on the nether surface of my chair. Your adventures, no doubt, are wonderful; but I don't successfully evoke them, understand them, believe in them. I do in those you write, heaven knows—but I don't in those you perform, though the latter, I know, are to lead to new revelations of the former and your capacity for them is certainly wonderful enough. This is a selfish personal cry: I wish you back; for literature is lonely and Bournemouth is barren without you. Your place in my affection has not been usurped by another—for there is not the least little scrap of another to usurp it. If there were I would perversely try to care for him. But there isn't—I repeat, and I literally care for nothing but your return. I haven't even your novel to stay my stomach withal. The wan wet months elapse and I see no sign of it. The beautiful portrait of your wife shimmers at me from my chimney-piece—brought some months ago by the natural McClure—but seems to refer to one as dim and distant and delightful as a 'toast' of the last century. I wish I could make you homesick—I wish I could spoil your fun. It is a very featureless time. The summer is rank with rheumatism—a dark, drowned, unprecedented season. The town is empty but I am not going away. I have no money, but I have a little work. I have lately written several short fictions—but you may not see them unless you come home. I have just begun a novel* which is to run through the *Atlantic* from January 1st and which I aspire to finish by the end of this year. In reality I suppose I shall not be fully delivered of it before the middle of next. After that, with God's help, I propose, for a longish period, to do nothing but short lengths. I want to leave a multitude of pictures of my time, projecting my small circular frame upon as many different spots as possible and going in for number as well as quality, so that the number may constitute a total having a certain value as observation and testimony. But there isn't so much as a creature here even to whisper such an intention to. Nothing lifts its hand in these islands save blackguard party politics. Criticism is of an abject density and puerility—it doesn't exist—it writes the intellect of our race too low. Lang, in the *D[aily] N[ews]*, every morning, and I believe in a hundred other places, uses his beautiful thin facility to write everything down to the lowest level of Philistine twaddle—the view of the old lady round the corner or the clever person at the dinner party. The incorporated society of authors (I belong to it, and so do you, I think, but I don't know what it is) gave a dinner the other night to American literati to thank them

* *The Tragic Muse.*

for praying for international copyright. I carefully forbore to go, thinking the gratulation premature, and I see by this morning's *Times* that the banquetted boon is further off than ever. Edmund Gosse has sent me his clever little life of Congreve, just out, and I have read it—but it isn't so good as his Raleigh. But no more was the insufferable subject. . . . Come, my dear Louis, grow not too thin. I can't question you—because, as I say, I don't conjure you up. You have killed the imagination in me—that part of it which formed your element and in which you sat vivid and near. Your wife and mother and Mr. Lloyd suffer also—I must confess it—by this failure of breath, of faith. Of course I have your letter—from Manasquan (is that the idiotic name?) of the—ingenuous me, to think there was a date! It was terribly impersonal—it did me little good. A little more and I shan't believe in you enough to bless you. Take this, therefore, as your last chance. I follow all with an aching wing, an inadequate geography and an ineradicable hope. Ever, my dear Louis, yours, to the last snub—

HENRY JAMES.

22

STEVENSON TO JAMES

Honolulu [*March*, 1889]

MY DEAR JAMES,

Yes—I own up—I am untrue to friendship and (what is less, but still considerable) to civilisation. I am not coming home for another year. There it is, cold and bald, and now you won't believe in me at all, and serve me right (says you) and the devil take me. But look here, and judge me tenderly. I have had more fun and pleasure of my life these past months than ever before, and more health than any time in ten long years. And even here in Honolulu I have withered in the cold; and this precious deep is filled with islands, which we may still visit; and though the sea is a deathful place, I like to be there, and like squalls (when they are over); and to draw near to a new island, I cannot say how much I like. In short, I take another year of this sort of life, and mean to try to work down among the poisoned arrows, and mean (if it may be) to come back again when the thing is through, and converse with Henry James as heretofore; and in the meanwhile issue directions to H. J. to write to me once more. Let him address here at Honolulu, for my views are vague; and if it is sent here it will follow and find me, if I am to be found; and if I am not to be found, the man James will have done his duty, and we shall be at the bottom of the sea, where no post-office clerk can be expected to discover us, or languishing on a coral island, the philosophic drudges of some barbarian potentate: perchance, of an American Missionary. My wife has just sent to Mrs. Sitwell a translation (*tant bien que mal*) of a letter I have had from my chief friend in this part of the world: go and see her, and get a hearing of it; it will do you good; it is a better method of correspondence than even Henry James's.* I jest, but seriously it

---

* The following is the letter in question:

'I make you to know my great affection. At the hour when you left us, I was filled with tears; my wife, Rui Telime, also, and all of my household. When you embarked I felt a great sorrow. It is for this that I went upon the road, and you looked from that ship, and I looked at you on the ship with great grief until you had raised the anchor and hoisted the sails. When the ship started I ran along the beach to see you still; and when you were on the open sea I cried out to you, "Farewell Louis"; and when I was coming back to my house I seemed to hear your voice crying "Rui farewell." Afterwards I watched the ship as long as I could until the night fell; and when it was dark I said to myself, If I had wings I should fly to the ship to meet you, and to sleep amongst you, so that I might be able to come back to shore and to tell Rui Telime, "I have slept upon the ship of Teriitera."

'After that we passed that night in the impatience of grief. Towards eight o'clock I seemed to hear your voice, "Teriitera—Rui—here is the hour for *putter* and *tiro*" (cheese and syrup). I did not sleep that night, thinking continually of you, my very dear friend, until the morning; being then still awake, I went to see Tapina Tutu on her bed, and alas, she was not there. Afterwards I looked into your rooms; they did not please me as they used to do. I did not hear your voice saying, "Hail Rui"; I thought then that you had gone, and that you had left me. Rising up, I went to the beach to see your ship, and I could not see it. I wept, then, until the night, telling myself continually, "Teriitera returns into his own country

is a strange thing for a tough, sick, middle-aged scrivener like R. L. S. to receive a letter so conceived from a man fifty years old, a leading politician, a crack orator, and the great wit of his village: boldly say, 'the highly popular M.P. of Tautira.' My nineteenth century strikes here, and lies alongside of something beautiful and ancient. I think the receipt of such a letter might humble, shall I say even———? and for me, I would rather have received it than written *Redgauntlet* or the sixth *Æneid*. All told, if my books have enabled or helped me to make this voyage, to know Rui, and to have received such a letter, they have (in the old prefatorial expression) not been writ in vain. It would seem from this that I have been not so much humbled as puffed up; but, I assure you, I have in fact been both. A little of what that letter says is my own earning; not all, but yet a little; and the little makes me proud, and all the rest ashamed; and in the contrast, how much more beautiful altogether is the ancient man than him of to-day!

Well, well, Henry James is pretty good, though he *is*

---

and leaves his dear Rui in grief, so that I suffer for him, and weep for him." I will not forget you in my memory. Here is the thought: I desire to meet you again. It is my dear Teriitera makes the only riches I desire in this world. It is your eyes that I desire to see again. It must be that your body and my body shall eat together at one table: there is what would make my heart content. But now we are separated. May God be with you all. May His word and His mercy go with you, so that you may be well and we also, according to the words of Paul.

    Ori A Ori, that is to say, Rui.'

of the nineteenth century, and that glaringly. And to curry favour with him, I wish I could be more explicit; but, indeed, I am still of necessity extremely vague, and cannot tell what I am to do, nor where I am to go for some while yet. As soon as I am sure, you shall hear. All are fairly well—the wife, your countrywoman, least of all; troubles are not entirely wanting; but on the whole we prosper, and we are all affectionately yours,

ROBERT LOUIS STEVENSON.

23

JAMES TO STEVENSON

34 De Vere Gardens, W.
April 29th, 1889

This is really dreadful news, my dear Louis, odious news to one who had neatly arranged that his coming August should be spent gobbling down your yarns—by some garden-window of Skerryvore—as the Neapolitan lazzarone puts away the lubricating filaments of the vermicelli. And yet, with my hideous capacity to understand it, I am strong enough, superior enough, to say *anything*, for conversation, later. It's in the light of unlimited conversation that I see the future years, and my honoured chair by the ingleside will require a succession of new cushions. I miss you shockingly—for, my dear fellow, there is no one—literally no one; and I don't in the least follow you—I can't go with you (I mean in conceptive faculty and the 'realising sense,') and you are for the time absolutely as if you were dead to me—I mean to my imagination of course—not to my affection or my prayers. And so I shall keep humble that you may pump into me—and make me stare and sigh and look simple and be quite out of it—for ever and ever. It's the best thing that can happen to one to see it written in your very hand that you have been so uplifted in health and cheer, and if another year will screw you up so tight that you won't 'come undone' again, I will try and hold on through the barren months. I will go to Mrs. Sitwell, to hear what has made you blush—it must be something very radical. Your chieftains are dim to me—why shouldn't they be when you yourself are? *Va* for another year—but don't stay away longer, for we should really, for self-defence, have to outlive you. . . . I myself do little but sit at home and write little tales—and even long ones—you shall see them when you come back. Nothing would induce me, by sending them to you, to expose myself to damaging Polynesian comparisons. For the rest, there is nothing in this land but the eternal Irish strife—the place is all gashed and gory with it. I can't tell you of it—I am too sick of it—more than to say that two or three of the most interesting days I ever passed were lately in the crowded, throbbing, thrilling little court of the Special Commission, over the astounding drama of the forged *Times* letters.

I have a hope, a dream, that your mother may be coming home and that one may go and drink deep of her narrations. But it's idle and improbable. A wonderful, beautiful letter from your wife to Colvin seemed, a few months ago, to make it clear that *she* has no quarrel with your wild and wayward life. I hope it agrees with her a little too—I mean that it renews her youth and strength. It is a woeful time to wait—for your prose as for your person—especially as the prose can't be better though the person may.

Your very faithful
HENRY JAMES.

24

STEVENSON TO JAMES

Union Club, Sydney, February 19th, 1890

HERE—in this excellent civilised, antipodal club smoking-room, I have just read the first part of your *Solution*.* Dear Henry James, it is an exquisite art; do not be troubled by the shadows of your French competitors: not one, not de Maupassant, could have done a thing more clean and fine; dry in touch, but the atmosphere (as in a fine summer sunset) rich with colour and with

* Published in the *New Review*, December 1889 to February 1890, and reprinted in *The Lesson of the Master* (1892).

perfume. I shall say no more; this note is De Solutione; except that I—that we—are all your sincere friends and hope to shake you by the hand in June.

ROBERT LOUIS STEVENSON.

signed, sealed and
delivered as his act
and deed
and very thought of very thought,
this nineteenth of February in the year of our
Lord one thousand eight hundred ninety
and nothing.

25

JAMES TO STEVENSON

34 De Vere Gardens, W.
March 21st, 1890

MY DEAR LOUIS AND MY DEAR MRS. LOUIS,

It comes over me with horror and shame that, within the next very few months, your return to England may become such a reality that I shall before long stand face to face with you branded with the almost blood-guilt of my long silence. Let me break that silence then, before the bliss of meeting you again (heaven speed the day) is qualified, in prospect, by the apprehension of your disdain. I despatch these incoherent words to Sydney, in the hope they may catch you before you embark for our palpitating England. My despicable dumbness has been a vile accident—I needn't assure you that it doesn't pretend to the smallest backbone of system or sense. I have simply had the busiest year of my life and have been so drained of the fluid of expression—so tapped into the public pitcher—that my whole correspondence has dried up and died of thirst. Then, somehow, you had become inaccessible to the mind as well as to the body, and I had the feeling that, in the midst of such desperate larks, any news of mine would be mere irrelevant drivel to you. Now, however, you *must* take it, such as it is. It won't, of course, be news to you at all that the idea of your return has become altogether the question of the day. The other two questions (the eternal Irish and Rudyard Kipling) aren't in it. (We'll tell you all about Rudyard Kipling— your nascent rival; he has killed one immortal—Rider Haggard; the star of the hour, aged 24 and author of remarkable Anglo-Indian and extraordinarily observed barrack life—Tommy Atkins—tales.) What I am pledged to do at the present moment (pledged to Colvin) is to plead with you passionately on the question of Samoa and expatriation. But somehow, when it comes to the point, I can't do it—partly because I can't really believe in anything so dreadful (a long howl of horror has gone up from all your friends), and partly because before any step so fatal is irretrievably taken we are to have a chance to see you and bind you with flowery chains.

When you tell me with your own melodious lips that you're committed, I'll see what's to be done; but I won't take a single plank of the house or a single hour of the flight for granted. Colvin has given me instantly all your recent unspeakable news—I mean the voyage to Samoa and everything preceding, and your mother has kindly communicated to me her own wonderful documents. Therefore my silence has been filled with sound—sound infinitely fearful sometimes. But the joy of your health, my dear Louis, has been to me as an imparted sensation —making me far more glad than anything that I could originate with myself. I shall never be as well as I am glad that you are well. We are poor tame, terrified products of the tailor and the parlour maid; but we have a fine sentiment or two, all the same. . . . I, thank God, am in better form than when you first took ship. I have lately finished the longest and most careful novel I have ever written* (it has gone 16 months in a periodical) and the last, in that form, I shall ever do—it will come out as a book in May. Also other things too flat to be bawled through an Australasian tube. But the intensest throb of my literary life, as of that of many others, has been *The Master of Ballantrae*—a pure hard crystal, my boy, a work of ineffable and exquisite art. It makes us all as proud of you as you can possibly be of *it*. Lead him on blushing, lead him back blooming, by the hand, dear Mrs. Louis, and we will talk over everything, as we used to lang syne at Skerryvore.

* *The Tragic Muse.*

When we *have* talked over everything and when all your tales are told, then you may paddle back to Samoa. But we shall call time. My heartiest greeting to the young Lloyd—grizzled, I fear, before his day. I have been very sorry to hear of your son-in-law's bad case. May all that tension be over now. *Do* receive this before you sail—*don't* sail till you get it. But then bound straight across. I send a volume of the Rising Star to goad you all hither with jealousy. He has quite done for your neglected even though neglectful friend,

HENRY JAMES.

26

JAMES TO STEVENSON

34 De Vere Gardens, W.
April 28th, 1890

MY DEAR LOUIS,

I didn't, for two reasons, answer your delightful letter, or rather exquisite note, from the Sydney Club, but I must thank you for it now, before the gulfs have washed you down, or at least have washed away from you all after-tastes of brineless things—the stay-at-home works of lubberly friends. One of the reasons just mentioned was that I had written to you at Sydney (c/o the mystic Towns,) only a few days before your note arrived; the other is that until a few days ago I hugged the soft illusion that by the time anything else would reach you, you would already have started for England. This fondest of hopes of all of us has been shattered in a manner to which history furnishes a parallel only in the behaviour of its most famous coquettes and courtesans. You are indeed the male Cleopatra or buccaneering Pompadour of the Deep—the wandering Wanton of the Pacific. You swim into our ken with every provocation and prospect—and we have only time to open our arms to receive you when your immortal back is turned to us in the act of still more provoking flight. The moral is that we have to be virtuous whether we like it or no. Seriously, it was a real heartbreak to have September substituted for June; but I have a general faith in the fascinated providence who watches over you, to the neglect of all other human affairs—I believe that even *He* has an idea that you know what you are about, and even what *He* is, though He by this time doesn't in the least know himself. Moreover, I have selfish grounds of resignation in the fact that I shall be in England in September, whereas, to my almost intolerable torment, I should probably not have been in June. Therefore when you come, if you ever do, which in my heart of hearts I doubt, I shall see you in all your strange exotic bloom, in all your paint and beads and feathers. May you grow a magnificent extra crop of all such things (as they will bring you a fortune here,) in this much grudged extra summer.

Charming and delightful to me to see you with a palate for *my* plain domestic pudding, after all the wild cannibal snacks that you have learned to know. I think the better of the poor little study in the painfully-familiar, since hearing that it could bear such voyages and resist such tests. You have fed a presumption that vaguely stirs within me—that of trying to get at you in June or July with a fearfully long-winded but very highly-finished novel which I am putting forth in (probably) the last days of May. If I were sure it would overtake you on some coral strand I shouldn't hesitate; for, seriously and selfishly speaking, I can't (spiritually) afford *not* to put the book under the eye of the sole and single Anglo-Saxon capable of perceiving—though he may care for little else in it— how well it is written. So I shall probably cast it upon the waters and pray for it; as I suppose you are coming back to Sydney, it may meet you there, and you can read it on the voyage home. In that box you'll *have* to. I don't say it to bribe you in advance to unnatural tolerance—but I have an impression that I didn't make copious or clear to you in my last what a grand literary life your *Master of B.* has been leading here. Somehow, a miracle has been wrought for you (for you they are,) and the fine old featherbed of English taste *has* thrilled with preternatural recognitions. The most unlikely number of people *have* discerned that *The Master* is 'well written.' It has had the highest success of honour that the English-reading public can now confer; where it has failed (the success, save that it hasn't failed at all!) it has done so through the constitutional incapacity of the umpire—infected, by vulgar intercourses, as with some unnameable disease. We have lost our status—*nous n'avons plus qualité*—to confer degrees. Nevertheless, last year you woke us up at night, for an hour—and we scrambled down in our shirt and climbed a garden-wall and stole a laurel, which we have been brandishing ever since over your absent head. I tell you this because I think Colvin (at least it was probably he—he is visibly better—or else Mrs. Sitwell) mentioned to me the other day that you had asked in touching virginal ignorance for news of the fate of the book. Its 'fate,' my dear fellow, has been glittering glory—simply: and I ween—that is I hope—you will find the glitter has chinked as well. I sent you a new Zola the other day—at a venture: but I have no confidence that I gratified a curiosity. I haven't read *The Human Beast*—one knows him without that—and I am told Zola's account of him is dull and imperfect. I would read anything new about him —but this is old, old, old. I hope your pen, this summer, will cleave the deeps of art even as your prow, or your keel, or whatever's the knowing name for it, furrows the Pacific flood. Into what strange and wondrous dyes you must be now qualified to dip it! Roast yourself, I beseech you, on the sharp spit of perfection, that you may give out your aromas and essences! Tell your wife, please, to read between the lines of this, and between the words and the letters, all that I miss the occasion to write directly to *her*. I hope she has continued to distil, to your mother, the honey of those impressions of which a few months ago the latter lent me for a day or two a taste—on its long yellow foolscap combs. They would make, they *will* make, of course, a deliciously sweet book. I hope Lloyd, whom I greet and bless, is living up to the height of his young privilege—and secreting honey too, according to the mild discipline of the hive. There are lots of things more to tell you, no doubt, but if I go on they will all take the shape of questions, and that won't be fair. The supreme thing to say is Don't, oh *don't*, simply ruin our nerves and our tempers for the rest of life by *not* throwing the rope in September, to him who will, for once in his life, not muff his catch:

H. J.

27

STEVENSON TO JAMES

Union Club, Sydney, August, 1890

MY DEAR HENRY JAMES,

Kipling is too clever to live. The *Bête Humaine* I had already perused in Noumea, listening the while to the strains of the convict band. He is a Beast; but not human, and, to be frank, not very interesting. 'Nervous maladies:

the homicidal ward,' would be the better name: O this game gets very tedious.

Your two long and kind letters have helped to entertain the old familiar sickbed. So has a book called *The Bondman*, by Hall Caine; I wish you would look at it. I am not half-way through yet. Read the book, and communicate your views. Hall Caine, by the way, appears to take Hugo's view of History and Chronology. (*Later;* the book doesn't keep up; it gets very wild.)

I must tell you plainly—I can't tell Colvin—I do not think I shall come to England more than once, and then it'll be to die. Health I enjoy in the tropics; even here, which they call sub- or semi-tropics, I come only to catch cold. I have not been out since my arrival; live here in a nice bedroom by the fireside, and read books and letters from Henry James, and send out to get his *Tragic Muse*, only to be told they can't be had as yet in Sydney, and have altogether a placid time. But I can't go out! The thermometer was nearly down to 50° the other day—no temperature for me, Mr. James: how should I do in England? I fear not at all. Am I very sorry? I am sorry about seven or eight people in England, and one or two in the States. And outside of that, I simply prefer Samoa. These are the words of honesty and soberness. (I am fasting from all but sin, coughing, *The Bondman*, a couple of eggs and a cup of tea.) I was never fond of towns, houses, society, or (it seems) civilisation. Nor yet it seems was I ever very fond of (what is technically called) God's green earth. The sea, islands, the islanders, the island life and climate, make and keep me truly happier. These last two years I have been much at sea, and I have *never wearied*; sometimes I have indeed grown impatient for some destination; more often I was sorry that the voyage drew so early to an end; and never once did I lose my fidelity to blue water and a ship. It is plain, then, that for me my exile to the place of schooners and islands can be in no sense regarded as a calamity.

Good-bye just now: I must take a turn at my proofs.

N.B. Even my wife has weakened about the sea. She wearied, the last time we were ashore, to get afloat again.

Yours ever,
R. L. S.

28

STEVENSON TO JAMES

Vailima, Apia, Samoa, December 29th, 1890

MY DEAR HENRY JAMES,

It is terrible how little everybody writes, and how much of that little disappears in the capacious maw of the Post Office. Many letters, both from and to me, I now know to have been lost in transit: my eye is on the Sydney Post Office, a large ungainly structure with a tower, as being not a hundred miles from the scene of disappearance; but then I have no proof. *The Tragic Muse* you announced to me as coming; I had already ordered it from a Sydney bookseller: about two months ago he advised me that his copy was in the post; and I am still tragically museless.

News, news, news. What do we know of yours? What do you care for ours? We are in the midst of the rainy season, and dwell among alarms of hurricanes, in a very unsafe little two-storied wooden box 650 feet above and about three miles from the sea-beach. Behind us, till the other slope of the island, desert forest, peaks, and loud torrents; in front green slopes to the sea, some fifty miles of which we dominate. We see the ships as they go out and in to the dangerous roadstead of Apia; and if they lie far out, we can even see their topmasts while they are at anchor. Of sounds of men, beyond those of our own labourers, there reach us, at very long intervals, salutes from the warships in harbour, the bell of the cathedral church, and the low of the conch-shell calling the labour boys on the German plantations. Yesterday, which was Sunday—the *quantième* is most likely erroneous; you can now correct it—we had a visitor—Baker of Tonga. Heard you ever of him? He is a great man here; he is accused of theft, rape, judicial murder, private poisoning, abortion, misappropriation of public moneys—oddly enough, not forgery, nor arson: you would be amused if you knew how thick the accusations fly in this South Sea world. I make no doubt my own character is something illustrious; or if not yet there is a good time coming.

But all our resources have not of late been Pacific. We have had enlightened society: La Farge the painter, and your friend Henry Adams: a great privilege—would it might endure. I would go oftener to see them, but the place is awkward to reach on horseback. I had to swim my horse the last time I went to dinner; and as I have not yet returned the clothes I had to borrow, I dare not return in the same plight: it seems inevitable—as soon as the wash comes in, I plump straight into the American consul's shirt or trousers! They, I believe, would come oftener to see me but for the horrid doubt that weighs upon our commissariat department; we have *often* almost nothing to eat; a guest would simply break the bank; my wife and I have dined on one avocado pear; I have several times dined on hard bread and onions. What would you do with a guest at such narrow seasons?—eat him? or serve up a labour boy fricasseed?

Work? work is now arrested, but I have written, I should think, about thirty chapters of the South Sea book*; they will all want rehandling, I daresay. Gracious, what a strain is a long book! The time it took me to design this volume, before I could dream of putting pen to paper, was excessive; and then think of writing a book of travels on the spot, when I am continually extending my in-

---

* *In the South Seas*, published serially during 1891 in the *New York Sun*, also in *Black and White*. 15 of the 35 Letters were privately printed in 1890 under the title *The South Seas*. All were included in the Edinburgh Edition (1896).

formation, revising my opinions, and seeing the most finely finished portions of my work come part by part in pieces. Very soon I shall have no opinions left. And without an opinion, how to string artistically vast accumulations of fact? Darwin said no one could observe without a theory; I suppose he was right; 'tis a fine point of metaphysics; but I will take my oath, no man can write without one—at least the way he would like to, and my theories melt, melt, melt, and as they melt the thaw-waters wash down my writing and leave residual tracts—wastes instead of cultivated farms.

Kipling is by far the most promising young man who has appeared since—ahem—I appeared. He amazes me by his precocity and various endowment. But he alarms me by his copiousness and haste. He should shield his fire with both hands 'and draw up all his strength and sweetness in one ball.' ('Draw all his strength and all his sweetness up into one ball'? I cannot remember Marvell's words.) So the critics have been saying to me; but I was never capable of—and surely never guilty of—such a debauch of production. At this rate his works will soon fill the habitable globe; and surely he was armed for better conflicts than these succinct sketches and flying leaves of verse? I look on, I admire, I rejoice for myself; but in a kind of ambition we all have for our tongue and literature I am wounded. If I had this man's fertility and courage, it seems to me I could heave a pyramid.

Well, we begin to be old fogies now; and it was high

time *something* rose to take our places. Certainly Kipling has the gifts; the fairy godmothers were all tipsy at his christening: what will he do with them?

I am going to manage to send a long letter every month to Colvin, which, I dare say, if it is ever of the least interest, he will let you see. My wife is now better, and I hope will be reasonably right. We are a very crazy couple to lead so rough a life, but we manage excellently: she is handy and inventive, and I have one quality, I don't grumble. The nearest I came was the other day: when I had finished dinner, I thought awhile, then had my horse saddled, rode down to Apia, and dined again—I must say with unblunted appetite; that is my best excuse. Goodbye, my dear James; find an hour to write to us, and register your letter. Yours affectionately,

R. L. S.

29

JAMES TO STEVENSON

34 *De Vere Gardens, W.*
January 12th, 1891

MY DEAR LOUIS,

I have owed you a letter too shamefully long—and now that I have taken my pen in hand, as we used to say, I feel how much I burn to communicate with you. As your magnanimity will probably have forgotten how long ago it was that you addressed me, from Sydney, the tragic statement of your permanent secession, I won't remind you of so detested a date. That statement, indeed, smote me to the silence I have so long preserved: I couldn't—I didn't protest; I even mechanically and grimly assented; but I couldn't *talk* about it—even to you and your wife. Missing you is always a perpetual ache—and aches are disqualifying for gymnastic feats. In short we forgive you (the Muses and the soft Passions forgive *us*!) but we can't quite *treat* you as if we did. However, all this while I have many things to thank you for. In the first place for Lloyd. He was delightful, we loved him—nous nous l'arrachâmes. He is a most sympathetic youth, and we revelled in his rich conversation and exclaimed on his courtly manners. How vulgar you'll think us all when you come back (there is malice in that 'when.') Then for the beautiful strange things you sent me and which make for ever in my sky-parlour a sort of dim rumble as of the Pacific surf. My heart beats over them—my imagination throbs—my eyes fill. I have covered a blank wall of my bedroom with an acre of painted cloth and feel as if I lived in a Samoan tent—and I have placed the sad sepia-drawing just where, 50 times a day, it most transports and reminds me. To-day what I am grateful for is your new ballad-book,* which has just reached me by your command. I have had time only to read the first

* *Ballads* (1891).

few things—but I shall absorb the rest and give you my impression of them before I close this. As I turn the pages I seem to see that they are full of charm and of your 'Protean' imaginative life—but above all of your terrible far-off-ness. My state of mind about that is of the strangest—a sort of delight at having you poised there in the inconceivable; and a miserable feeling, at the same time, that I am in too wretched a back seat to assist properly at the performance. I don't want to lose *any* of your vibrations; and, as it is, I feel that I only catch a few of them—and that is a constant woe. I read with unrestrictive relish the first chapters of your prose volume* (kindly vouchsafed me in the little copyright-catching red volume,) and I loved 'em and blessed them quite. But I *did* make one restriction—I missed the *visible* in them—I mean as regards people, things, objects, faces, bodies, costumes, features, gestures, manners, the introductory, the *personal* painter-touch. It struck me that you either didn't feel—through some accident—your responsibility on this article quite enough; or, on some theory of your own, had declined it. No theory is kind to us that cheats us of *seeing*. However, no doubt we shall rub our eyes for satiety before we have done. Of course the pictures—Lloyd's blessed photographs—y sont pour beaucoup; but I wanted more the note of portraiture. Doubtless I am greedy—but one *is* when one dines at the Maison d'Or. I have an idea you take but a qualified interest in

* The privately printed edition of *The South Seas* (1890).

Beau Austin—or I should tell you how religiously I was present at that memorable première. Lloyd and your wonderful and delightful mother will have given you the agreeable facts of the occasion. I found it—not the occasion, so much, but the work—full of *quality*, and stamped with a charm; but on the other hand seeming to shrug its shoulders a little too much at scenic precautions. I have an idea, however, you don't care about the matter, and I won't bore you with it further than to say that the piece has been repeatedly played, that it has been the only honourable affair transacted dans notre sale tripot for many a day—and that Wm. Archer *en raffole* periodically in the *World*. Don't despise me too much if I confess that *anch' io son pittore*. Je fais aussi du théâtre, moi; and am doing it, to begin with, for reasons too numerous to burden you with, but all excellent and practical. In the provinces I had the other night, at Southport, Lancashire, with the dramatization of an early novel—*The American* —a success dont je rougis encore. This thing is to be played in London only after several months—and to make the tour of the British Islands first. Don't be hard on me—simplifying and chastening necessity has laid its brutal hand on me and I have had to try to make somehow or other the money I don't make by literature. My books don't sell, and it looks as if my plays might. Therefore I am going with a brazen front to write half a dozen. I have, in fact, already written two others than the one just performed; and the success of the latter pronounced—really *pronounced*—will probably precipitate them. I am glad for all this that you are not here. Literature is out of it. I miss no occasion of talking of you. Colvin I tolerably often see: I expect to do so for instance to-night, at a decidedly too starched dining-club to which we both belong, of which Lord Coleridge is president and too many persons of the type of Sir Theodore Martin are members. Happy islanders—with no Sir Theodore Martin. On Mrs. Sitwell I called the other day, in a charming new habitat: all clean paint and fresh chintz. We always go on at a great rate about you—celebrate rites as faithful as the early Christians in the catacombs. . . .

January 13th.—I met Colvin last night, after writing the above—in the company of Sir James Stephen, Sir Theo. Martin, Sir Douglas Galton, Sir James Paget, Sir Alfred Lyall, Canon Ainger, and George du Maurier. How this will make you lick your chops over Ori and Rahiro and Tamatia and Taheia—or whatever ces messieurs et ces dames, your present visiting list, are called. He told me of a copious diary-letter he has just got from you, bless you, and we are discussing a day on which I shall soon come to meat or drink with him and listen to the same. Since yesterday I have also read the ballad book —with the admiration that I always feel as a helplessly verseless creature (it's a sentiment worth nothing as a testimony) for all performances in rhyme and metre— especially on the part of producers of fine prose.

January 19th.—I stopped this more than a week ago,

and since then I have lacked time to go on with it—having been out of town for several days on a base theatrical errand—to see my tribute to the vulgarest of the muses a little further on its way over the provincial circuit and re-rehearse two or three portions of it that want more effective playing. Thank heaven I shall have now no more direct contact with it till it is produced in London next October.—I broke off in the act of speaking to you about your ballad-book. The production of ringing and lilting verse (by a superior proser) always does *bribe* me a little—and I envy you in that degree yours; but apart from this I grudge your writing the like of these ballads. They show your 'cleverness,' but they don't show your genius. I should say more if it were not odious to a man of my refinement to write to you—so expectantly far away—in remonstrance. I don't find, either, that the cannibalism, the savagery *se prête*, as it were—one wants either less of it, on the ground of suggestion—or more, on the ground of statement; and one wants more of the high impeccable (as distinguished from the awfully jolly,) on the ground of poetry. Behold I *am* launching across the black seas a page that may turn nasty—but, my dear Louis, it's only because I love so your divine prose and want the comfort of it. Things are various because we do 'em. We mustn't do 'em because they're various. The only news in literature here—such is the virtuous vacancy of our consciousness—continues to be the infant monster of a Kipling. I enclose, in this, for your entertainment a few pages I have lately written about him, to serve as the preface to an (of course authorized) American *recueil* of some of his tales.* I may add that he has just put forth his longest story yet—a thing in *Lippincott*† which I also send you herewith—which cuts the ground somewhat from under my feet, inasmuch as I find it the most youthfully infirm of his productions (in spite of great 'life',) much wanting in composition and in narrative and explicative, or even implicative, art.

Please tell your wife, with my love, that all this is constantly addressed to her also. I try to see you all, in what I fear is your absence of habits, as you live, grouped around what I also fear is in no sense the domestic hearth. Where do you go when you want to be 'cosy'? —or what at least do you *do*? You think a little, I hope, of the faithful forsaken on whose powers of evocation, as well as of attachment, you impose such a strain. I wish I could send a man from Fortnum and Mason's out to you with a chunk of *mortadella*. I am trying to do a series of 'short things' and will send you the least bad. I mean to write to Lloyd. Please congratulate your heroic mother for me very cordially when she leaps upon your strand, and believe that I hold you all in the tenderest remembrance of yours ever, my dear Louis,

HENRY JAMES.

* *Mine Own People* (1891).
† *The Light That Failed*, issue of January 1891.

30

JAMES TO STEVENSON

34 De Vere Gardens, W.
February 18th, 1891

MY DEAR LOUIS,

Your letter of December 29th is a most touching appeal; I am glad my own last had been posted to you 2 or 3 weeks before it reached me. Whether mine has—or will have been—guided to your coral strand is a matter as to which your disclosures touching the state of the Samoan post inspire me with the worst apprehensions. At any rate I did despatch you—supposedly via San Francisco—a really pretty long screed about a month ago. I ought to write to you all the while; but though I seem to myself to live with my pen in my hand I achieve nothing capable of connecting me so with glory. I am going to Paris to-morrow morning for a month, but I have vowed that I will miss my train sooner than depart without scrawling you and your wife a few words to-night. I shall probably see little or nothing there that will interest you much (or even interest myself hugely—) but having neither a yacht, an island, an heroic nature, a gallant wife, mother and son, nor a sea-stomach, I have to seek adventure in the humblest forms. In writing the other day I told you more or less what I was doing—*am* doing—in these elderly days; and the same general description will serve. I am doing what I can to launch myself in the dramatic direction—and the strange part of the matter is that I am doing it more or less seriously, as if we *had* the Scène Anglaise which we haven't. And I secretly dream of supplying the vile want? Pas même—and my zeal in the affair is only matched by my indifference. What is serious in it is that having begun to work in this sense some months ago, to give my little ones bread—I find the *form* opens out before me as if there were a kingdom to conquer —a kingdom forsooth of ignorant brutes of managers and dense cabotins of actors. All the same, I feel as if I had at last *found* my form—my real one—that for which pale fiction is an ineffectual substitute. God grant this unholy truth may not abide with me more than two or three years —time to dig out eight or ten rounded masterpieces and make withal enough money to enable me to retire in peace and plenty for the unmolested business of a *little* supreme writing, as distinguished from gouging—which is the Form above-mentioned. Your loneliness and your foodlessness, my dear Louis, bring tears to my eyes. If there were only a parcels' post to Samoa I would set Fortnum and Mason to work at you at this end of the line. But if they intercept the hieroglyphics at Sydney, what would they do to the sausage? Surely there is some cure for your emptiness; if nothing else, why not coming away? Don't eat up Mrs. Louis, whatever you do. You are precious to literature—but she is precious to the affections, which are larger, yet in a still worse way.... I shall certainly do my utmost to get to Egypt to see you, if, as is hinted to me by dear Colvin, you turn up there after the fitful fever of Samoa. Your being there would give me wings—especially if plays should give me gold. This is an exquisitely blissful dream. Don't fail to do your part of it. I almost joy in your lack of *The Tragic Muse*; as proving to me, I mean, that you are curious enough to have missed it. Nevertheless I have just posted to you, registered, the first copy I have received of the 1 vol. edition; but this moment out. I wanted to send you the three volumes by Lloyd, but he seemed clear you would have received it, and I didn't insist, as I knew he was charged with innumerable parcels and bales. I will presently send another *Muse*, and one, at least, must reach you.... Colvin is really better, I think—if any one can be better who is so absolutely good. I hope to God my last long letter will have reached you. I promise to write soon again. I enfold you all in my sympathy and am ever your faithfullest

HENRY JAMES.

31

STEVENSON TO JAMES

[*Vailima, Samoa, October*, 1891]

MY DEAR HENRY JAMES,

From this perturbed and hunted being expect but a line, and that line shall be but a whoop for Adela.* O she's delicious, delicious; I could live and die with Adela—die, rather the better of the two; you never did a straighter thing, and never will.

David Balfour, second part of *Kidnapped*, is on the stocks at last; and is not bad, I think. As for *The Wrecker*, it's a machine, you know—don't expect aught else—a machine, and a police machine; but I believe the end is one of the most genuine butcheries in literature; and we point to our machine with a modest pride, as the only police machine without a villain. Our criminals are a most pleasing crew, and leave the dock with scarce a stain upon their character.

What a different line of country to be trying to draw Adela, and trying to write the last four chapters of *The Wrecker*! Heavens, it's like two centuries; and ours is such rude, transpontine business, aiming only at a certain

* This heroine of James's short story *The Marriages* (published in the *Atlantic Monthly*, August 1891, and later included in *The Lesson of the Master*) is fascinating because of her well-meaning awfulness rather than for any more conventional charms.

fervour of conviction and sense of energy and violence in the men; and yours is so neat and bright and of so exquisite a surface! Seems dreadful to send such a book to such an author; but your name is on the list. And we do modestly ask you to consider the chapters on the *Norah Creina* with the study of Captain Nares, and the forementioned last four, with their brutality of substance and the curious (and perhaps unsound) technical manœuvre of running the story together to a point as we go along, the narrative becoming more succinct and the details fining off with every page.

Sworn affidavit of R. L. S.

No person now alive has beaten Adela: I adore Adela and her maker. Sic subscrib.

ROBERT LOUIS STEVENSON.

A Sublime Poem to follow.

> Adela, Adela, Adela Chart,
> What have you done to my elderly heart?
> Of all the ladies of paper and ink
> I count you the paragon, call you the pink.
>
> The word of your brother depicts you in part:
> 'You raving maniac!' Adela Chart;
> But in all the asylums that cumber the ground,
> So delightful a maniac was ne'er to be found.
>
> I pore on you, dote on you, clasp you to heart,
> I laud, love, and laugh at you, Adela Chart,
> And thank my dear maker the while I admire
> That I can be neither your husband nor sire.

> Your husband's, your sire's were a difficult part;
> You're a byway to suicide, Adela Chart;
> But to read of, depicted by exquisite James,
> O, sure you're the flower and quintessence of dames.
>
> R. L. S.

Eructavit cor meum

My heart was inditing a goodly matter about Adela Chart.

> Though oft I've been touched by the volatile dart,
> To none have I grovelled but Adela Chart,
> There are passable ladies, no question, in art—
> But where is the marrow of Adela Chart?
> I dreamed that to Tyburn I passed in the cart—
> I dreamed I was married to Adela Chart:
> From the first I awoke with a palpable start,
> The second dumbfoundered me, Adela Chart!

Another verse bursts from me, you see; no end to the violence of the Muse.

32

STEVENSON TO JAMES

[Vailima, Samoa] December 7th, 1891

MY DEAR HENRY JAMES,

Thanks for yours; your former letter was lost; so it appears was my long and masterly treatise on *The Tragic Muse*. I remember sending it very well, and there went by the same mail a long and masterly tractate to Gosse about his daddy's life, for which I have been long expecting an acknowledgment, and which is plainly gone to the bottom with the other. If you see Gosse, please mention it. These gems of criticism are now lost literature, like the tomes of Alexandria. I could not do 'em again. And I must ask you to be content with a dull head, a weary hand, and short commons, for to-day, as I am physically tired with hard work of every kind, the labours of the planter and the author both piled upon me mountain deep. I am delighted beyond expression by Bourget's book:* he has phrases which affect me almost like Montaigne; I had read ere this a masterly essay of his on Pascal; this book does it; I write for all his essays by this mail, and shall try to meet him when I come to Europe. The proposal is to pass a summer in France, I think in Royat, where the faithful could come and visit me; they are now not many. I expect Henry James to come and break a crust or two with us. I believe it will be only my wife and myself; and she will go over to England, but not I, or possibly incog. to Southampton, and then to Boscombe to see poor Lady Shelley. I am writing—trying to write in a Babel fit for the bottomless pit; my wife, her daughter, her grandson and my mother, all shrieking at each other round the house— not in war, thank God! but the din is ultra martial, and the note of Lloyd joins in occasionally, and the cause of this to-do is simply cacao, whereof chocolate comes. You may drink of our chocolate perhaps in five or six years

* *Sensations d'Italie.*

from now, and not know it. It makes a fine bustle, and gives us some hard work, out of which I have slunk for to-day.

I have a story coming out: God knows when or how; it answers to the name of *The Beach of Falesá*, and I think well of it. I was delighted with *The Tragic Muse*; I thought the Muse herself one of your best works; I was delighted also to hear of the success of your piece,* as you know I am a dam failure, and might have dined with the dinner club that Daudet and these parties frequented.

Next day. I have just been breakfasting at Baiae and Brindisi, and the charm of Bourget hag-rides me. I wonder if this exquisite fellow, all made of fiddle-strings and scent and intelligence, could bear any of my bald prose. If you think he could, ask Colvin to send him a copy of these last essays of mine when they appear; and tell Bourget they go to him from a South Sea Island as literal homage. I have read no new book for years that gave me the same literary thrill as his *Sensations d'Italie*. If (as I imagine) my cut-and-dry literature would be death to him, and worse than death—journalism—be silent on the point. For I have a great curiosity to know him, and if he doesn't know my work, I shall have the better chance of making his acquaintance. I read *The Pupil* the other day with great joy; your little boy is admirable; why is there no little boy like that unless he hails from the Great Republic?

* A dramatization of *The American*.

Here I broke off, and wrote Bourget a dedication;* no use resisting; it's a love affair. O, he's exquisite, I bless you for the gift of him. I have really enjoyed this book as I— almost as I—used to enjoy books when I was going twenty—twenty-three; and these are the years for reading!

R. L. S.

33

JAMES TO STEVENSON

34 De Vere Gardens, W.
March 19th, 1892

MY DEAR LOUIS,

I send you to-day by book-post, registered, a little volume of tales† which I lately put forth—most of which however you may have seen in magazines. Please accept at any rate the modest offering. Accept, too, my thanks for your sweet and dateless letter which I received a month ago—the one in which you speak with such charming appreciation and felicity of Paul Bourget. I echo your admiration—I think the Italian book one of the most exquisite things of our time. I am in only very occasional correspondence with him—and have not written since I heard from you; but I shall have an early

---

* To the volume of essays, *Across the Plains* (1892).
† *The Lesson of the Master.* See Letter No. 35.

chance, now probably, to repeat your words to him, and they will touch him in a tender place. He is living much, now, in Italy, and I may go there for May or June—though indeed I fear it is little probable. Colvin tells me of the volume of some of your *inédites* beauties that is on the point of appearing, and the news is a bright spot in a vulgar world. The vulgarity of literature in these islands at the present time is not to be said, and I shall clutch at you as one turns one's ear to music in the clatter of the market-place. Yet, paradoxical as it may appear, oh Louis, I have still had the refinement not to read *The Wrecker* in the periodical page. This is an enlightened and judicious heroism, and I do as I would be done by. Trust me, however, to taste you in long draughts as soon as I can hold the book. Then will I write to you again. You tell me nothing of yourself—so I have nothing to take up or take hold of, save indeed the cherished superstition that you enjoy some measure of health and cheer. You are, however, too far away for my imagination, and were it not for dear Colvin's friendly magic, which puts in a pin here and there, I shouldn't be able to catch and arrest at all the opaline iridescence of your legend. Yet even when he speaks of intending wars and the clash of arms, it all passes over me like an old-time song. You see how much I need you close at hand to stand successfully on the tiptoe of emulation. You fatigue, in short, my credulity, though not my affection. We lately clubbed together, all, to despatch to you an eye-witness in the person of the genius or the *genus*, in himself, Rudyard, for the concussion of whose extraordinary personality with your own we are beginning soon to strain the listening ear. We devoutly hope that this time he will really be washed upon your shore.* With him goes a new little wife —whose brother—Wolcott Balestier, lately dead, in much youthful promise and performance (I don't allude, in saying that, especially to the literary part of it,) was a very valued young friend of mine. . . . The main thing that has lately happened to myself is the death of my dear sister a fortnight ago—after years of suffering, which, however, had not made her any less rare and remarkable a person or diminished the effect of the event (when it should occur) in making an extreme difference in my life. Of my occupation what shall I tell you? I have of late years left London less and less—but I am thinking sooner or later (in a near present) of making a long foreign, though not distant, absence. I am busy with the *short*—I have forsworn the long. I hammer at the horrid little theatrical problem, with delays and intermissions, but, horrible to relate, no failure of purpose. I shall soon publish another small story-book which I will incontinently send you. I have done many brief fictions within the last year. . . . The good little Thomas Hardy has scored a great success with *Tess of the d'Urbervilles*, which is chock-full of faults and falsity and yet has a singular beauty and charm. . . .

  * Kipling did not pay his projected visit to Samoa.

What we most talk of here, however, is the day when it may be believed that you will come to meet us on some attainable southern shore. We will *all* go to the Mediterranean for you—let that not nail you to Samoa. I send every greeting to your play-fellows—your fellow-phantoms. The wife-phantom knows my sentiments. The ghost of a mother has my heartiest regard. The long Lloyd-spectre laughs an eerie laugh, doubtless, at my [word illegible] embrace. Yet I feel, my dear Louis, that I *do* hold you just long enough to press you to the heart of your very faithful old friend,

HENRY JAMES.

34

JAMES TO STEVENSON

34 De Vere Gardens, W.
April 15th, 1892

MY DEAR LOUIS,

I send you by this post the magnificent *Mémoires de Marbot*, which should have gone to you sooner by my hand if I had sooner read them and sooner, thereby, grasped the idea of how much they would probably beguile for you the shimmering tropical noon. The three volumes go to you in three separate registered book-post parcels and all my prayers for an escape from the queer perils of the way attend and hover about them. Some people, I believe, consider this fascinating warrior a bien-conditionné Munchausen—but perish the injurious thought. Me he not only charms but convinces. I can't manage a letter, my dear Louis, to-day—I wrote you a longish one, via San Francisco (like this,) just about a month ago. But I mustn't fail to tell you that I have just read the last page of the sweet collection of some of your happiest lucubrations put forth by the care of dear Colvin.* They make a most desirable, and moreover a very honourable, volume. It was indispensable to bring them together and they altogether justify it. The first one, and *The Lantern-Bearers* and two last, are of course the best—these last are all made up of high and admirable pages and do you the greatest credit. You have never felt, thought, said, more finely and happily than in many a passage here, and are in them altogether at your best. I don't see reviews or meet newspapers now (beside which the work is scarcely in the market,) so I don't know what fortune the book encounters—but it is enough for me—I admit it can hardly be enough for you—that I love it. I pant for the completion of *The Wrecker*—of which Colvin unwove the other night, to my rapturous ear, the weird and wondrous tangle. I hope I don't give him away if I tell you he even read me a very interesting letter from you—though studded with critical stardust in which I a little lost my way—telling of a project of a dashing roman de

* *Across the Plains.*

mœurs all about a wicked woman.* For this you may imagine how I yearn—though not to the point of wanting it before the sequel of *Kidnapped*. For God's sake let me have them both. I marvel at the liberality of your production and rejoice in this high meridian of your genius. I leave London presently for 3 or 4 months—I wish it were with everything required for leaping on your strand. Sometimes I think I have got through the worst of missing you and then I find I haven't. I pine for you as I pen these words, for I am more and more companionless in my old age—more and more shut up to the solitude inevitably the portion, in these islands, of him who would really try, even in so small a way as mine, to *do* it. I'm often on the point of taking the train down to Skerryvore, to serenade your ghosts, get them to throw a fellow a word. Consider this, at any rate, a plaintive invocation. Again, again I greet your wife, that lady of the closed lips, and I am yours, my dear Louis, and Lloyd's and your mother's undiscourageably,

HENRY JAMES.

* Stevenson outlined his projected novel, *Sophia Scarlet*, in a letter to Colvin on January 31st, 1892

35

STEVENSON TO JAMES

*[Vailima] December 5th, 1891**

MY DEAR JAMES,

How comes it so great a silence has fallen? The still small voice of self-approval whispers me it is not from me. I have looked up my register, and find I have neither written to you nor heard from you since June 22nd, on which day of grace that invaluable work began. This is not as it should be. How to get back? I remember acknowledging with rapture *The Lesson of the Master*, and I remember receiving *Marbot*: was that our last relation?

Hey, well! anyway, as you may have probably gathered from the papers, I have been in devilish hot water, and (what may be new to you) devilish hard at work. In twelve calendar months I finished *The Wrecker*, wrote all of *Falesá* but the first chapter, (well, much of) the *History of Samoa*, did something here and there to my Life of my Grandfather, and began And Finished *David Balfour*. What do you think of it for a year? Since then I may say I have done nothing beyond draft three chapters of another novel, *The Justice-Clerk*,† which ought to be a snorter and a blower—at least if it don't make a spoon,

---
* Actually 1892. See Letter No. 36.
† The original title of *Weir of Hermiston*.

it will spoil the horn of an Aurochs (if that's how it should be spelt).

On the hot water side it may entertain you to know that I have been actually sentenced to deportation by my friends on Mulinuu, C. J. Cedercrantz and Baron Senfft von Pilsach. The awful doom, however, declined to fall, owing to Circumstances over Which. I only heard of it (so to speak) last night. I mean officially, but I had walked among rumours. The whole tale will be some day put into my hand, and I shall share it with humorous friends.

It is likely, however, by my judgment, that this epoch of gaiety in Samoa will soon cease; and the fierce white light of history will beat no longer on Yours Sincerely and his fellows here on the beach. We ask ourselves whether the reason will more rejoice over the end of a disgraceful business, or the unregenerate man more sorrow over the stoppage of the fun. For, say what you please, it has been a deeply interesting time. You don't know what news is, nor what politics, nor what the life of man, till you see it on so small a scale and with your own liberty on the board for stake. I would not have missed it for much. And anxious friends beg me to stay at home and study human nature in Brompton drawing-rooms! *Farceurs!* And anyway you know that such is not my talent. I could never be induced to take the faintest interest in Brompton *qua* Brompton or a drawing-room *qua* a drawing-room. I am an Epick Writer with a k to it, but without the necessary genius.

Hurry up with another book of stories. I am now reduced to two of my contemporaries, you and Barrie—O, and Kipling—you and Barrie and Kipling are now my Muses Three. And with Kipling, as you know, there are reservations to be made. And you and Barrie don't write enough. I should say I also read Anstey when he is serious, and can almost get a happy day out of Marion Crawford—*ce n'est pas toujours la guerre*, but it's got life to it and guts, and it moves. Did you read *The Witch of Prague*? Nobody could read it twice, of course; and the first time even it was necessary to skip. *E pur si muove*. But Barrie is a beauty, *The Little Minister* and the *Window in Thrums*, eh? Stuff in that young man; but he must see and not be too funny. Genius in him, but there's a journalist at his elbow—there's the risk. Look, what a page is the glove business in the *Window*! knocks a man flat; that's guts, if you please.*

Why have I wasted the little time that is left with a sort of naked review article? I don't know, I'm sure. I suppose a mere ebullition of congested literary talk. I am beginning to think a visit from friends would be due. Wish you could come!

Let us have your news anyway, and forgive this silly stale effusion.

    Yours ever,
     ROBERT LOUIS STEVENSON.

* Barrie, in *An Edinburgh Eleven* (1888), wrote rather patronisingly of both Stevenson and James.

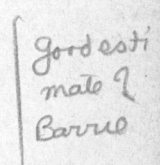

36

JAMES TO STEVENSON

34 *De Vere Gardens, W.*
February 17th, 1893

MY DEAR DISTANT LOUIS,

The charmingest thing that had happened to me for a year was the advent of your reassuring note of Dec. 5th (not 1891—my dear time-deluded islander: it is enviable to see you so luxuriously 'out.' When you indulge in the eccentricity of a date you make it eccentric indeed.) I call your good letter reassuring simply on the general ground of its making you credible for an hour. You are otherwise wholly of the stuff that dreams are made of. I think this is why I don't keep writing to you, don't talk to you, as it were, in my sleep. Please don't think I forget you or am indifferent to anything that concerns you. The mere thought of you is better company than almost any that is tangible to me here, and London is more peopled to me by your living in Samoa than by the residence of almost anybody else in Kensington or Chelsea. I fix my curiosity on you all the while and try to understand your politics and your perils and your public life. If in these efforts I make a poor figure it is only because you are so wantonly away. Then I think I envy you too much— your climate, your thrill of life, your magnificent facility. You judge well that I have far too little of this last—

though you *can't* judge how much more and more difficult I find it every day to write. None the less I am presently putting forth, almost with exact simultaneity, three little (distinct) books—2 volumes of penny fiction and one of little essays,* all material gathered, no doubt, from sources in which you may already have encountered some of it. However this may be, the matter shall again be (D.V.) deposited on your coral strand. Most refreshing, even while not wholly convincing, was the cool trade-wind (is the trade-wind cool?) of your criticism of some of *ces messieurs*. I grant you Hardy with all my heart. . . . I am meek and ashamed where the public clatter is deafening—so I bowed my head and let *Tess of the D.'s* pass. But oh yes, dear Louis, she is vile. The pretence of 'sexuality' is only equalled by the absence of it, and the abomination of the language by the author's reputation for style. There are indeed some pretty smells and sights and sounds. But you have better ones in Polynesia. On the other hand I can't go with you three yards in your toleration either of —— or of ——.† Let me add that I can't read them, so I don't know anything about them. All the same I make no bones to pronounce them shameless *industriels* and their works only glories of Birmingham. You will have gathered that I delight in your year of literary prowess. None the less I haven't read a word of

* *The Real Thing*, *The Private Life*, and *Essays in London and Elsewhere*, all published in 1893.
† Presumably Anstey and Marion Crawford. See Letter No. 35.

you since the brave and beautiful *Wrecker*. I won't *touch* you till I can feel that I embrace you in the embracing cover. So it is that I languish till the things now announced appear. Colvin makes me impatient for *David Balfour*—but doesn't yet stay my stomach with the *Beach of Falesá*. . . . Mrs. Sitwell *me fait part* of every savoury scrap she gets from you. I know what you all magnificently eat, and what dear Mrs. Louis splendidly (but not somewhat transparently—no?) wears. Please assure that intensely-remembered lady of my dumb fidelity. I am told your mother nears our shores and I promise myself joy on seeing her and pumping her. I don't know, however, alas, how long this ceremony may be delayed, as I go to Italy, for all the blessed spring, next week. I have been in London without an hour's absence since the middle of August last. I hear you utter some island objurgation, and go splashing, to banish the stuffy image, into the sapphire sea. Is it all a fable that you will come some month to the Mediterranean? I would go to the Pillars of Hercules to greet you. Give my love to the lusty and literary Lloyd. I am very glad to observe him spreading his wings. There is absolutely nothing to send you. The Muses are dumb, and in France as well. Of Bourget's big 7 franc *Cosmopolis* I have, alas, purchased three copies —and given them away; but even if I were to send you one you would find it too round and round the subject— which heaven knows it is—for your taste. I will try and despatch you the charming little *Etui de Nacre* of Anatole France—a real master. Vale—ave. Yours, my dear Louis, in a kind of hopeful despair and a clinging alienation,

HENRY JAMES.

37

STEVENSON TO JAMES

[Vailima, Samoa, May 19th, 1893]

MY DEAR JAMES,

This is going to you by the hands of our cousin, Graham Balfour—who will tell you all about us—and how we do, and what we don't—and the Tamaitai's Garden and generally the ins and outs of our way of life. You will find him a first rate fellow.

Yours ever,
ROBERT LOUIS STEVENSON.

38

STEVENSON TO JAMES

*Vailima Plantation, Samoan Islands,
June 17th, 1893*

MY DEAR HENRY JAMES,

I believe I have neglected a mail in answering yours. You will be very sorry to hear that my wife was exceedingly ill, and very glad to hear that she is better. I cannot say that I feel any more anxiety about her. We shall send you a photograph of her taken in Sydney in her customary island habit as she walks and gardens and shrilly drills her brown assistants. She was very ill when she sat for it, which may a little explain the appearance of the photograph. It reminds me of a friend of my grandmother's who used to say when talking to younger women, 'Aweel, when I was young I wasnae just exactly what ye wad call *bonny*, but I was pale, penetratin', and interestin'.' I would not venture to hint that Fanny is 'no bonny,' but there is no doubt but that in this presentment she is 'pale, penetratin', and interestin'.'

As you are aware, I have been wading deep waters and contending with the great ones of the earth, not wholly without success. It is, you may be interested to hear, a dreary and infuriating business. If you can get the fools to admit one thing, they will always save their face by denying another. If you can induce them to take a step to the right hand, they generally indemnify themselves by cutting a caper to the left. I always held (upon no evidence whatever, from a mere sentiment or intuition) that politics was the dirtiest, the most foolish, and the most random of human employments. I always held, but now I know it! Fortunately, you have nothing to do with anything of the kind, and I may spare you the horror of further details.

I received from you a book by a man by the name of

Anatole France. Why should I disguise it? I have no use for Anatole. He writes very prettily, and then afterwards? Baron Marbot was a different pair of shoes. So likewise is the Baron de Vitrolles, whom I am now perusing with delight. His escape in 1814 is one of the best pages I remember anywhere to have read. But Marbot and Vitrolles are dead, and what has become of the living? It seems as if literature were coming to a stand. I am sure it is with me; and I am sure everybody will say so when they have the privilege of reading *The Ebb-Tide*. My dear man, the grimness of that story is not to be depicted in words. There are only four characters, to be sure, but they are such a troop of swine! And their behaviour is really so deeply beneath any possible standard, that on a retrospect I wonder I have been able to endure them myself until the yarn was finished. Well, there is always one thing; it will serve as a touchstone. If the admirers of Zola admire him for his pertinent ugliness and pessimism, I think they should admire this; but if, as I have long suspected, they neither admire nor understand the man's art, and only wallow in his rancidness like a hound in offal, then they will certainly be disappointed in *The Ebb-Tide*. Alas! poor little tale, it is not *even* rancid.

By way of an antidote or febrifuge, I am going on at a great rate with my History of the Stevensons, which I hope may prove rather amusing, in some parts at least. The excess of materials weighs upon me. My Grandfather is a delightful comedy part; and I have to treat him besides as a serious and (in his way) a heroic figure, and at times I lose my way, and I fear in the end will blur the effect. However, *à la grâce de Dieu!* I'll make a spoon or spoil a horn. You see, I have to do the Building of the Bell Rock by cutting down and packing my grandsire's book, which I rather hope I have done, but do not know. And it makes a huge chunk of a very different style and quality between Chapters II. and IV. And it can't be helped! It is just a delightful and exasperating necessity. You know the stuff is really excellent narrative; only, perhaps there's too much of it! There is the rub. Well, well, it will be plain to you that my mind is affected; it might be with less. *The Ebb-Tide* and *Northern Lights** are a full meal for any plain man.

I have written and ordered your last book, *The Real Thing*, so be sure and don't send it. What else are you doing or thinking of doing? News I have none, and don't want any. I have had to stop all strong drink and all tobacco, and am now in a transition state between the two, which seems to be near madness. You never smoked, I think, so you can never taste the joys of stopping it. But at least you have drunk, and you can enter perhaps into my annoyance when I suddenly find a glass of claret or a brandy-and-water give me a splitting headache the next morning. No mistake about it; drink anything, and there's your headache. Tobacco just as bad for me. If I live

* Eventually published in the Edinburgh Edition (1896) as *A Family of Engineers*.

through this breach of habit, I shall be a white-livered puppy indeed. Actually I am so made, or so twisted, that I do not like to think of a life without the red wine on the table and the tobacco with its lovely little coal of fire. It doesn't amuse me from a distance. I may find it the Garden of Eden when I go in, but I don't like the colour of the gate-posts. Suppose somebody said to you, you are to leave your home, and your books, and your clubs, and go out and camp in mid-Africa, and command an expedition, you would howl, and kick, and flee. I think the same of a life without wine and tobacco; and if this goes on, I've got to go and do it, sir, in the living flesh!

I thought Bourget was a friend of yours? And I thought the French were a polite race? He has taken my dedication with a stately silence that has surprised me into apoplexy. Did I go and dedicate my book to the nasty alien, and the 'norrid Frenchman, and the Bloody Furrineer? Well, I wouldn't do it again; and unless his case is susceptible of explanation, you might perhaps tell him so over the walnuts and the wine, by way of speeding the gay hours. Sincerely, I thought my dedication worth a letter.

If anything be worth anything here below! Do you know the story of the man who found a button in his hash, and called the waiter? 'What do you call that?' says he. 'Well,' said the waiter, 'what d'you expect? Expect to find a gold watch and chain?' Heavenly apologue, is it not? I expected (rather) to find a gold watch and chain;

I expected to be able to smoke to excess and drink to comfort all the days of my life; and I am still indignantly staring on this button! It's not even a button; it's a teetotal badge!

Ever yours,
ROBERT LOUIS STEVENSON.

39

JAMES TO STEVENSON

34 De Vere Gardens, W.
[*Summer* 1893]

*... I seem to be making phrases, my dear Stevenson, when in reality I am thinking of you with the simple longing of my helplessness to aid. It may well be, however, I take it, that the conditions are by this time better and the future brighter—and for such a consummation I heartily pray.—Thanks to my absence from England I wholly missed your mother—a few weeks ago—when she was in London. The nearest I came to seeing her was corresponding earnestly and elegantly with a kinswoman

* This fragment of a letter consists of four pages on a double sheet of notepaper, with the ending and postscript written vertically in the margins. Two pages are reproduced here.

It is undated, but the references to the *Island Nights' Entertainments*, to the forthcoming publication in book form of *David Balfour* (the title under which *Catriona* ran as a serial) and to the visit of Mrs. Thomas Stevenson, place it in the summer of 1893.

34, De Vere Gardens. W.

I seem to be making phrases, my dear Stevenson, when in reality I am thinking of you with the simple longing of my helplessness to aid. It may well be, however, I take it, that by this time the conditions are a better and the future brighter — & for such a consummation I heartily pray. — Thanks to my absence from England I

faithfullest remembrances to your wife & to Lloyd.

the system. The art of "The Beach of Falesâ" seems to me an art brought to a perfection — I delight in the observed truth, the modesty of nature, of the narrator. Primitive man doesn't interest me, I confess, as much as civilized — and yet he does, when you write about him. However, a part of my impatience for "David Balfour" to become a book held in the hand and caressed by the eyes, springs from the apprehension that

of yours with whom she was staying. It was a disappointment of magnitude, so pressingly am I disposed to question her. But the chance will come, as I learn with joy that she is to be here many months. It was only when I came back the other day that I could put my hand on the *Island Nights*, which by your generosity (please be tenderly thanked,) I found awaiting me on my table. They have for me all the same old charm, and I read them as fondly as an infant sucks a stick of candy. Fortunately, unlike the candy they are still there after sucking—to be freshly reabsorbed into the system. The art of *The Beach of Falesá* seems to me an art brought to a perfection and I delight in the observed truth, the modesty of nature, of the narrator. Primitive man doesn't interest me, I confess, as much as civilized—and yet he *does*, when you write about him. However, a part of my impatience for *David Balfour* to become a book held in the hand and caressed by the eyes, springs from the apprehension that . . .

For yourself, my dear Louis, I grasp your hand and am yours always,

HENRY JAMES.

Faithfullest remembrances to your wife and to Lloyd.

40

STEVENSON TO JAMES

Apia, July, 1893

MY DEAR HENRY JAMES,

Yes. *Les Trophées** is, on the whole, a book. It is excellent; but is it a life's work? I always suspect *you* of a volume of sonnets up your sleeve; when is it coming down? I am in one of my moods of wholesale impatience with all fiction and all verging on it, reading instead, with rapture, *Fountainhall's Decisions*.† You never read it: well, it hasn't much form, and is inexpressibly dreary, I should suppose, to others—and even to me for pages. It's like walking in a mine underground, and with a damned bad lantern, and picking out pieces of ore. This, and war, will be my excuse for not having read your (doubtless) charming work of fiction. The revolving year will bring me round to it; and I know, when fiction shall begin to feel a little *solid* to me again, that I shall love it, because it's James. Do you know, when I am in this mood, I would rather try to read a bad book? It's not so disappointing, anyway. And *Fountainhall* is prime, two big folio volumes, and all dreary, and all true, and all as terse as an obituary; and about one interesting fact on an average in

* By José-Maria de Hérédia.
† Fountainhall's *Decisions of the Lords of Council*, which Stevenson had been reading as background material for *St. Ives, Weir of Hermiston,* and other projected Scottish novels.

twenty pages, and ten of them unintelligible for technicalities. There's literature, if you like! It feeds; it falls about you genuine like rain. Rain: nobody has done justice to rain in literature yet: surely a subject for a Scot. But then you can't do rain in that ledger-book style that I am trying for—or between a ledger-book and an old ballad. How to get over, how to escape from, the besotting *particularity* of fiction. 'Roland approached the house; it had green doors and window blinds; and there was a scraper on the upper step.' To hell with Roland and the scraper! Yours ever,

R. L. S.

41
JAMES TO STEVENSON

34 De Vere Gardens, W.
August 5th, 1893

MY DEAR LOUIS,

I have a most charming and interesting letter, and a photographic representation of your fine head which I cannot so unrestrictedly commend, to thank you for. The portrait has its points as a memento, but they are not fine points as a likeness. I remember you, I think of you, I evoke you, much more plastically. But it was none the less liberal and faithful of you to include me in the list of fond recipients. Your letter contained all sorts of good things, but best of all the happy news of your wife's better condition. I rejoice in that almost obstreperously and beg you to tell her so with my love. The Sydney photograph that you kindly announce (of her) hasn't come, but I impatiently desire it. Meanwhile its place is gracefully occupied by your delightful anecdote of your mother's retrospective Scotch friend—the pale, penetratin' and interestin' one. Perhaps you will permit me to say that it is exquisitely Scotch; at any rate it moves altogether in the highest walks of anecdote.

I get, habitually, the sympathetic infection, from Colvin, of so much general uneasiness and even alarm about you, that it is reassuring to find you apparently incommoded by nothing worse than the privation of liquor and tobacco. 'Nothing worse?' I hear you echo, while you ask to what more refined savagery of torture I can imagine you subjected. You would rather perhaps—and small blame to you—perish by the sword than by famine. But you won't perish, my dear Louis, and I am here to tell you so. *I* should have perished—long ago—if it were mortal. No liquor—to speak of—passes my wasted lips, and yet they are capable of the hypocrisy of the sigh of resignation. I am very, very sorry for you—for I remember the genial tray which in the far-off, fabulous time used to be placed, as the evening waxed, under the social lamp at Skerryvore. The evenings wax at Vailima, but the tray, I gather, has waned. May this heavy trial be lightened, and, as you missionaries say, be even blessed to you. It wounds, I repeat, but it doesn't kill—more's the pity. The tobacco's another question. I have smoked a cigarette—at Skerryvore; and I shall probably smoke one again. But I don't look forward to it. However, you will think me objectionably destitute of temperament. What depresses me much more is the sad sense that you receive scarcely anything I send you. This, however, doesn't deter me from posting you to-day, registered, via San Francisco (it is post-day,) a volume of thin trifles lately put forth by me and entitled *Essays in London and Elsewhere*. It contains some pretty writing—not addressed to the fishes. My last letter to you, to which yours of June 17th [was a reply]—the only dated one, dear Louis, I ever got from you!—was intended to accompany two other volumes of mine, which were despatched to you, registered, via San F., at the same moment (*The Real Thing* and *The Private Life*). Yet neither of these works, evidently, had reached you when you ask me not to send you the former (though my letter mentioned that it had started,) as you had ordered it. It is all a mystery which the fishes only will have sounded. I also post to you herewith Paul Bourget's last little tale (*Un Scrupule*,) as to which nothing will induce me to utter the faintest rudiments of an opinion. It is full of talent (I don't call *that* a rudiment,) but the French are passing strange. I am very glad to be able to send you herewith enclosed a *petit mot* from the said Paul Bourget, in response to your sense of outrage at his too-continuous silence. . . . His intentions, I can answer for it, had been the best; but he leads so migratory a life that I don't see how *any* intention can ever well fructify. He has spent the winter in the Holy Land and jumps thence in three weeks (from Beyrout) to his queer American expedition. A year ago—more—he earnestly asked me (at Siena) for your address. I as eagerly gave it to him—par écrit—but the acknowledgment that he was then full of the desire to make to you succumbed to complex frustrations. Now that, at last, here it is, I wish you to be able to *read* it! But you won't. My hand is the hand of Apollo to it.

I have been at the sea-side for six weeks, and am back in the empty town mainly because it *is* empty. *My* seaside is the sordid sands of Ramsgate—I see your coral-reefs blush pink at the vulgarity of the name. The place has for me an unutterable advantage (in the press of working-weeks) which the beach of Falesá would, fortunately, *not* have—that of being full of every one I don't know. The beach of Falesá would enthrall but sterilize me—I mean the social muse would disjoint the classic nose of the other. You will certainly think me barren enough as I am. I am really less desiccated than I seem, however, for I am working with patient subterraneity at a trade which it is dishonour enough to practise, without talking about it: a trade supremely dangerous and heroically difficult—*that* credit at least belongs to it. The case is simplified for me by the direst necessity: the *book*, as my limitations compel me to produce it, doesn't bring me in a penny. Tell it not in Samoa—or at least not in Tahiti; but I *don't* sell ten copies!—and neither editors nor publishers will have anything whatever to say to me. But I never mention it—nearer home. 'Politics,' dear politician—I rejoice that you are getting over them. When you say that you always 'believed' them beastly I am tempted to become superior and say that I always knew them so. At least I don't see how one can have glanced, however cursorily, at the contemporary newspapers (I mean the journal of one's whole time,) and had any doubt of it. The morals, the manners, the materials of all those gentlemen are writ there more large than any record is elsewhere writ, and the impudence of their airs and pretensions in the presence of it revolts even the meekness of a spirit as resigned to everything as mine. The sordid fight in the House of Commons the other night seemed to me only a momentary intermission of hypocrisy. The hypocrisy comes back with the pretended confusion over it. The Lives of the Stevensons (with every respect to them) isn't what I want you most to write, but I would rather you should publish ten volumes of them than another letter to *The Times*.* Meanwhile I am languishing for *Catriona*—and the weeks follow and I must live without you. It isn't life. But I am still amicably yours and your wife's and the insidious Lloyd's,

HENRY JAMES.

* Stevenson wrote letters to *The Times* on Samoan affairs which appeared on June 4th, July 23rd, Aug. 19th and Oct. 17th, 1892.

42

JAMES TO STEVENSON

34 De Vere Gardens, W.
October 21st [1893]

MY DEAR LOUIS,

The postal guide tells me, disobligingly, that there is no mail to you via San Francisco this month and that I must confide my few lines to the precarious and perfidious Hamburg. I do so, then, for the plain reason that I can no longer repress the enthusiasm that has surged within me ever since I read *Catriona*. I missed, just after doing so, last month's post, and I was infinitely vexed that it should not have conveyed to you the freshness of my rapture. For the said *Catriona* so reeks and hums with genius that there is no refuge for the desperate reader but in straightforward prostration. I'm not sure that it's magnanimous of you to succeed so inconsiderately—there is a modesty in easy triumph which your flushed muse perhaps a little neglects.—But forgive that lumbering image—I won't attempt to carry it out. Let me only say that I don't despatch these ineffectual words on their too watery way to do anything but thank you for an exquisite pleasure. I hold that when a book has the high beauty of that one there's a poor indelicacy in what simple folk call criticism. The work lives by so absolute a law that it's grotesque to prattle about what *might* have been! I shall express to you the one point in which my sense was conscious of an unsatisfied desire, but only after saying first how rare an achievement I think the whole personality and tone of David and with how supremely happy a hand you have coloured the palpable women. They are quite too lovely and everyone is running after them. In David not an error, not a false note ever; he is all of an exasperating truth and rightness. The one thing I miss in the book is the note of *visibility*—it subjects my visual sense, my *seeing* imagination, to an almost painful underfeeding. The *hearing* imagination, as it were, is nourished like an alderman, and the loud audibility seems a slight the more on the baffled lust of the eyes—so that I seem to myself (I am speaking of course only from the point of view of the way, as I read, *my* impression longs to complete itself) in the presence of voices in the darkness—voices the more distinct and vivid, the more brave and sonorous, as voices always are—but also the more tormenting and confounding—by reason of these bandaged eyes. I utter a pleading moan when you, e.g., transport your characters, toward the end, in a line or two from Leyden to Dunkirk without the glint of a hint of all the ambient picture of the 18th century road. However, stick to your own system of evocation so long as what you positively achieve is so big. Life and letters and art all take joy in you.

I am rejoiced to hear that your wife is less disturbed in health and that your anxieties are somewhat appeased. I don't know how sufficiently to renew, to both of you, the assurance of all my friendliest sympathy. You live in conditions so unimaginable and to the tune of experience so great and so strange that you must forgive me if I am altogether out of step with your events. I know you're surrounded with the din of battle, and yet the beauty you produce has the Goethean calm, even like the beauty distilled at Weimar when the smoke was over Jena. Let me touch you at least on your bookish side and the others may bristle with heroics. I pray you be made accessible some day in a talkative armchair by the fire. If it hadn't been for *Catriona* we couldn't, this year, have held up our head. It had been long, before that, since any decent sentence was turned in English. We grow systematically vulgarer and baser. The only blur of light is that your books are tasted. I shall try to see Colvin before I post this—otherwise I haven't seen him for three months. I've had a summer of the British seaside, the bathing machine and the German band. I met Zola at luncheon the day before he left London and found him very sane and common and inexperienced. Nothing, literally nothing, has ever happened to him but to write the *Rougeon-Macquart*. It makes that series, I admit, still more curious. Your tour de force is of the opposite kind. Renew the miracle, my dear Louis, and believe me yours already gaping,

HENRY JAMES.

P.S. I have had to keep my poor note several days

—finding that after all there *is*, thank heaven, a near post by San Francisco. Meanwhile I have seen Colvin and made discreetly, though so eagerly, free of some of your projects—and gyrations! Trapezist in the Pacific void!

... *Catriona* is more and more BEAUTIFUL. There's the rub!

H. J.

43

STEVENSON TO JAMES

Apia, December, 1893

MY DEAR HENRY JAMES,

The mail has come upon me like an armed man three days earlier than was expected; and the Lord help me! It is impossible I should answer anybody the way they should be. Your jubilation over *Catriona* did me good, and still more the subtlety and truth of your remark on the starving of the visual sense in that book. 'Tis true, and unless I make the greater effort—and am, as a step to that, convinced of its necessity—it will be more true I fear in the future. I *hear* people talking, and I *feel* them acting, and that seems to me to be fiction. My two aims may be described as—

    1st.   War to the adjective.
    2nd.   Death to the optic nerve.

Admitted we live in an age of the optic nerve in literature. For how many centuries did literature get along without a sign of it? However, I'll consider your letter.

How exquisite is your character of the critic in *Essays in London*! I doubt if you have done any single thing so satisfying as a piece of style and of insight.

Yours ever,
R. L. S.

44

STEVENSON TO JAMES

Vailima, July 7th, 1894

DEAR HENRY JAMES,

I am going to try and dictate to you a letter or a note, and begin the same without any spark of hope, my mind being entirely in abeyance. This malady is very bitter on the literary man. I have had it now coming on for a month, and it seems to get worse instead of better. If it should prove to be softening of the brain, a melancholy interest will attach to the present document. I heard a great deal about you from my mother and Graham Balfour; the latter declares that you could take a First in any Samoan subject. If that be so, I should like to hear you on the theory of the constitution. Also to consult you on the force of the particles *o lo'o* and *ua*, which are the subject of a dispute among local pundits. You might, if you ever answer this, give me your opinion on the origin of the Samoan race, just to complete the favour.

They both say that you are looking well, and I suppose I may conclude from that that you are feeling passably. I wish I was. Do not suppose from this that I am ill in body; it is the numskull that I complain of. And when that is wrong, as you must be very keenly aware, you begin every day with a smarting disappointment, which is not good for the temper. I am in one of the humours when a man wonders how any one can be such an ass as to embrace the profession of letters, and not get apprenticed to a barber or keep a baked-potato stall. But I have no doubt in the course of a week, or perhaps to-morrow, things will look better.

We have at present in port the model war-ship of Great Britain. She is called the *Curaçoa*, and has the nicest set of officers and men conceivable. They, the officers, are all very intimate with us, and the front verandah is known as the Curaçoa Club, and the road up to Vailima is known as the Curaçoa Track. It was rather a surprise to me; many naval officers have I known, and somehow had not learned to think entirely well of them, and perhaps sometimes ask myself a little uneasily how that kind of men could do great actions? and behold! the answer comes to me, and I see a ship that I would guarantee to go anywhere it was possible for men to go, and accomplish anything it was permitted man to attempt. I had a cruise on board of her not long ago to Manu'a, and was delighted. The good-will of all on board; the grim playfulness of [word missing] quarters, with the wounded falling down at the word; the ambulances hastening up and carrying them away; the Captain suddenly crying, 'Fire in the ward-room!' and the squad hastening forward with the hose; and, last and most curious spectacle of all, all the men in their dust-coloured fatigue clothes, at a note of the bugle, falling simultaneously flat on deck, and the ship proceeding with its prostrate crew—*quasi* to ram an enemy; our dinner at night in a wild open anchorage, the ship rolling almost to her gunwales, and showing us alternately her bulwarks up in the sky, and then the wild broken cliffy palm-crested shores of the island with the surf thundering and leaping close aboard. We had the ward-room mess on deck, lit by pink wax tapers, everybody, of course, in uniform but myself, and the first lieutenant (who is a rheumaticky body) wrapped in a boat cloak. Gradually the sunset faded out, the island disappeared from the eye, though it remained menacingly present to the ear with the voice of the surf, and then the captain turned on the searchlight and gave us the coast, the beach, the trees, the native houses, and the cliffs by glimpses of daylight, a kind of deliberate lightning. About which time, I suppose, we must have come as far as the dessert, and were probably drinking our first glass of port to her Majesty. We stayed two days at the island, and had, in addition, a very picturesque snapshot at the native life. The three islands of Manu'a are independent, and are ruled over by a little slip of a half-caste girl about twenty, who sits all day in a pink gown, in a little white European house with about a quarter of an acre of roses in front of it, looking at the palm-trees on the village street, and listening to the surf. This, so far as I could discover, was all she had to do. 'This is a very dull place,' she said. It appears she could go to no other village for fear of raising the jealousy of her own people in the capital. And as for going about 'tafatafaoing,' as we say here, its cost was too enormous. A strong able-bodied native must walk in front of her and blow the conch shell continuously from the moment she leaves one house until the moment she enters another. Did you ever blow the conch shell? I presume not; but the sweat literally hailed off that man, and I expected every moment to see him burst a blood-vessel. We were entertained to kava in the guest-house with some very original features. The young men who run for the kava have a right to misconduct themselves *ad libitum* on the way back; and though they were told to restrain themselves on the occasion of our visit, there was a strange hurly-burly at their return, when they came beating the trees and the posts of the houses, leaping, shouting, and yelling like Bacchants.

I tasted on that occasion what it is to be great. My name was called next after the captain's, and several chiefs (a thing quite new to me, and not at all Samoan practice) drank to me by name.

And now, if you are not sick of the *Curaçoa* and Manu'a, I am, at least on paper. And I decline any longer to give you examples of how not to write.

By the by, you sent me long ago a work by Anatole France, which I confess I did not *taste*. Since then I have made the acquaintance of *Abbé Coignard*, and have become a faithful adorer. I don't think a better book was ever written.

And I have no idea what I have said, and I have no idea what I ought to have said, and I am a total ass, but my heart is in the right place, and I am, my dear Henry James, yours,

R. L. S.

45

STEVENSON TO JAMES

Vailima, Samoa.
November 24th, 1894

MY DEAR JAMES,

Will you allow me to introduce to you my young friend Mr. C. D. Burney, whom we have had the pleasure to see much of here in Samoa? We saw him go with regret, and it seems to break the separation if we hand him on to friends in England. Apply to him for details of my four o'clock in the morning cocoa.

> Yours ever,
> ROBERT LOUIS STEVENSON.

46

JAMES TO FANNY STEVENSON*

[*December* 1894]

MY DEAR FANNY STEVENSON,

What can I say to you that will not seem cruelly irrelevant or vain? We have been sitting in darkness for nearly a fortnight, but what is our darkness to the extinction of your magnificent light? You will probably know in some degree what has happened to us—how the hideous news first came to us via Auckland, etc., and then how, in the newspapers, a doubt was raised about its authenticity—just enough to give one a flicker of hope; until your telegram to me via San Francisco—repeated also from other sources—converted my pessimistic convictions into the wretched knowledge. All this time my thoughts have hovered round you all, around you in particular, with a tenderness of which I could have wished you might have, afar-off, the divination. You are such a visible picture of desolation that I need to remind myself

* Stevenson died suddenly in Samoa on December 3rd, 1894.

that courage, and patience, and fortitude are also abundantly with you. The devotion that Louis inspired—and of which all the air about you must be full—must also be much to you. Yet as I write the word, indeed, I am almost ashamed of it—as if anything could be 'much' in the presence of such an abysmal void. To have lived in the light of that splendid life, that beautiful, bountiful thing —only to see it, from one moment to the other, converted into a fable as strange and romantic as one of his own, a thing that has been and has ended, is an anguish into which no one can enter fully and of which no one can drain the cup for you. You are nearest to the pain, because you were nearest the joy and the pride. But if it is anything to you to know that no woman was ever more felt with and that your personal grief is the intensely personal grief of innumerable hearts—know it well, my dear Fanny Stevenson, for during all these days there has been friendship for you in the very air. For myself, how shall I tell you how much poorer and shabbier the whole world seems, and how one of the closest and strongest reasons for going on, for trying and doing, for planning and dreaming of the future, has dropped in an instant out of life. I was haunted indeed with a sense that I should never again see him—but it was one of the best things in life that he was there, or that one had him—at any rate one heard of him, and felt him and awaited him and counted him into everything one most loved and lived for. He lighted up one whole side of the globe, and was in himself a whole province of one's imagination. We are smaller fry and meaner people without him. I feel as if there was a certain indelicacy in saying it to you, save that I know that there is nothing narrow or selfish in your sense of loss —for himself, however, for his happy name and his great visible good fortune, it strikes one as another matter. I mean that I feel him to have been as happy in his death (struck down that way, as by the gods, in a clear, glorious hour) as he had been in his fame. And, with all the sad allowances in his rich full life, he had the best of it—the thick of the fray, the loudest of the music, the freshest and finest of himself. It isn't as if there had been no full achievement and no supreme thing. It was all intense, all gallant, all exquisite from the first, and the experience, the fruition, had something dramatically complete in them. He has gone in time not to be old, early enough to be so generously young and late enough to have drunk deep of the cup. There have been—I think—for men of letters few deaths more romantically right. Forgive me, I beg you, what may sound cold blooded in such words—or as if I imagined there could be anything for you 'right' in the rupture of such an affection and the loss of such a presence. I have in my mind in that view only the rounded career and the consecrated work. When I think of your own situation I fall into a mere confusion of pity and wonder, with the sole sense of your being as brave a spirit as he was (all of whose bravery you shared) to hold on by. Of what solutions or decisions you see before you we shall hear in time; meanwhile please believe that I am most affectionately with you.... More than I can say, I hope your first prostration and bewilderment are over, and that you are feeling your way in feeling all sorts of encompassing arms—all sorts of outstretched hands of friendship. Don't, my dear Fanny Stevenson, be unconscious of mine, and believe me more than ever faithfully yours,

HENRY JAMES.

47

THE LETTERS OF ROBERT LOUIS STEVENSON*

BY HENRY JAMES

It was the happy fortune of Robert Louis Stevenson to have created, beyond any man of his craft in our day, a body of readers inspired with the feelings that we, for the most part, place at the service only of those for whom our affection is personal. There was no one who knew the man, one may safely assert, who was not also devoted to the writer; conforming in this respect to a general law—if law it be—that shows us many exceptions: but, naturally and not inconveniently, it had to remain far from true that all devotees of the writer were able to approach the

* A review of *Letters to His Family and Friends*, edited by Sidney Colvin (1899). This article was first published in the *North American Review*, January 1900, and was reprinted in *Notes on Novelists* (1914).

man. The case was, nevertheless, that the man, somehow, approached *them*, and that to read him—certainly to read him with the full sense of his charm—came, for many people, to mean much the same as to 'meet' him. It was as if he wrote himself altogether, rose straight to the surface of his prose, and still more of his happiest verse; so that these things gave out, besides whatever else, his look and his voice, showed his life and manners, his affairs and his very secrets. In short, we grew to possess him entire; and the example is the more curious and beautiful, as he neither made a business of 'confession' nor cultivated most of those forms through which the *ego* shines. His great successes were supposititious histories of persons quite different from himself, and the objective, as we have learned to call it, was the ideal to which he oftenest sacrificed.

The effect of it all, none the less, was such that his Correspondence has only seemed to administer, delightfully, a further push to a door already half open and through which we enter with an extraordinary absence of the sense of intrusion. We feel, indeed, that we are living with him; but what is that but what we were doing before? Through his Correspondence, indeed, the *ego* does, magnificently, shine—which is much the best thing that, in any correspondence, it can ever do. But even the *Vailima Letters*, published by Mr. Sidney Colvin in 1895, had already both established that and allayed our diffidence.

'It came over me the other day suddenly that this diary of mine to you would make good pickings after I am dead, and a man could make some kind of book out of it without much trouble. So, for God's sake, don't lose them.'

Being on these terms with our author, and feeling as if we had always been, we profit by freedoms that seem but the consecration of intimacy. Not only have we no sense of intrusion, but we are so prepared to penetrate further that when we come to limits we quite feel as if the story were mutilated and the copy not complete. There it is precisely that we seize the secret of our tie. Of course, it was personal, for how did it operate, in any connection whatever, but to make us live with him? We had lived with him in *Treasure Island*, in *Kidnapped* and in *Catriona*, just as we do, by the light of these posthumous volumes, in the South Seas and at Vailima; and our present confidence comes from the fact of a particularly charming continuity. It is not that his novels were 'subjective,' but that his life was romantic, and in the very same degree in which his own conception, his own presentation, of that element touches and thrills. If we want to know even more, it is because we are always, everywhere, in the story.

To this absorbing extension of the story, then, the two volumes of *Letters* now published by Mr. Sidney Colvin beautifully contribute. The shelf of our library that contains our best letter-writers is considerably furnished, but not overcrowded; and its glory is not too great to keep

Stevenson from finding there a place with the very first. He will not figure among the writers—those to whom we are apt to give, in this line, precedence—to whom only small things happen, and who fascinate us by making the most of them; he belongs to the class who have both matter and manner, whom life carries swiftly before it, and who communicate and signal as they go. He lived to the topmost pulse; and the last thing that was to happen was that he should find himself, on any occasion, with nothing to recount. Of all that he may have uttered on certain occasions, we are, inevitably, not here possessed —a fact that, as I have hinted above, affects us, perversely, as an inexcusable gap in the story; but he never fails of the thing that we most love letters for, the full expression of the moment and the mood, the actual good or bad or middling, the thing in his head, his heart or his house. Mr. Colvin has given us an admirable 'Introduction'—a characterization of his friend so founded at once on knowledge and on judgment that the whole sense of the man strikes us as extracted in it. He has elucidated each group or period with notes that leave nothing to be desired; and nothing remains, that I can think of, to thank him for, unless the intimation that we may yet look for another volume—which, however much more free it might make us of the author's history, we should accept, I repeat, with the same absence of scruple. Nothing comes up oftener to-day than the question of the rights of privacy; of our warrant, or want of warrant, for getting behind, by the aid of editors or other retailers, certain appearances of distinction; and the general knot in the business is, indeed, a hard one to untie; yet it strikes me as a matter regarding which such publications as Mr. Colvin's have much to suggest.

There is no absolute privacy—save, of course, when the deceased may have wished or endeavoured positively to constitute it; and things too sacred are often only things that are not, in that degree, anything else that is superior. One may hold both that people—that artists perhaps in particular—are well advised to cover their tracks, and yet that our having gone, or not, behind, in a particular case, may be a small affair compared with our having really found something. Personal records of the type before us can, at any rate, obviously, be but the reverse of a deterrent to the pushing inquirer. They are too happy an instance—they positively make for revelations. Stevenson never covered his tracks, and the tracks prove, perhaps, to be what most attaches us. We follow them here, from year to year and from stage to stage, with the same charmed sense with which he has made us follow one of his hunted heroes in the heather. Life and fate and an early catastrophe were ever at his heels, and when he at last falls fighting, sinks down in the very act of valour, the 'happy ending,' as he calls it for some of his correspondents, is, though precipitated and not conventional, assuredly there.

His descent and his origin all contribute to the picture,

which, it seems to me, could scarce—since we speak of 'endings'—have had a better beginning had he himself prearranged it. Without his having prearranged it, indeed, it was such a matter as could never be wasted on him, one of the innumerable things, Scotch and other, that helped to fill his romantic consciousness. Edinburgh, in the first place, the 'romantic town,' was as much his 'own' as it ever was the great precursor's whom, in *Weir of Hermiston* as well as elsewhere, he presses so hard; and this even in spite of continual absence—in virtue of a constant, imaginative reference and an intense, intellectual possession. The immediate background formed by the profession of his family—the charge of the lights on northern coasts—was a setting that he could not have seen his way to better; while no less happy a condition was met by his being all lonely in his father's house—the more that the father, admirably commemorated by the son and in his way as strongly marked, was antique and strenuous, and that the son, a genius to be, and delicate, was (in the words of the charming anecdote of an Edinburgh lady retailed in one of these volumes), if not exactly what could be called bonny, 'pale, penetrating and interesting.' The poet in him had, from the first, to be pacified—temporarily, that is, and from hand to mouth, as is the way for poets; so that, with friction and tension playing their part, with the filial relation quite classically troubled, with breaks of tradition and lapses from faith, with restless excursions and sombre returns, with the love of life at large mixed, in his heart, with every sort of local piety and passion, and the unjustified artist fermenting, on top of all, in the recusant engineer, he was as well started as possible toward the character he was to keep.

All this, obviously, however, was the sort of thing that the story, as most generally approved, would have had at heart to represent as the mere wild oats of a slightly uncanny cleverness—as handsomely reconciled, in time, to the usual scheme and crowned, after an amusing fling or two, with young wedded love and civic responsibility. The actual story, alas, was to transcend the conventional one, for it happened to be a case of a hero of too long a wind and too well turned out for his part. Everything was right for the discipline of Alan Fairford, but that the youth *was*, after all, a phœnix. As soon as it became a case of justifying himself for straying—as in the enchanting *Inland Voyage* and *Travels with a Donkey*—how was he to escape doing so with supreme felicity? The fascination in him, from the first, is the mixture, and the extraordinary charm of his letters is that they are always showing this. It is the proportions, moreover, that are so admirable—the quantity of each different thing that he fitted to each other one, and to the whole. The free life would have been all his dream, if so large a part of it had not been that love of letters, of expression and form, which is but another name for the life of service. Almost the last word about him, by the same law, would be that he had, at any rate, supremely written, were it not that he seems still better characterized by his having at any rate supremely lived.

Perpetually and exquisitely amusing as he was, his ambiguities and compatibilities yielded, for all the wear and tear of them, endless 'fun' even to himself; and no one knew so well with what linked diversities he was saddled, or—to put it the other way—how many horses he had to drive at once. It took his own delightful talk to show how more than absurd it might be, and, if convenient, how very obscurely so, that such an incurable rover should have been complicated both with such an incurable scribbler and such an incurable invalid, and that a man should find himself such an anomaly as a drenched yachtsman haunted with 'style,' a shameless Bohemian haunted with duty, and a victim at once of the personal hunger and instinct for adventure and of the critical, constructive, sedentary view of it. He had everything all round—adventure most of all; to feel which we have only to turn from the beautiful flush of it in his text to the scarce less beautiful vision of the great hilltop in Pacific seas to which, after death, he was borne by islanders and chiefs. Fate, as if to distinguish him as handsomely as possible, seemed to be ever treating him to some chance for an act or a course that had almost nothing in its favour but its inordinate difficulty. If the difficulty was, in these cases, not *all* the beauty for him, it at least never prevented his finding in it—or our finding, at any rate, as observers—so much beauty as comes from a great risk accepted either for an idea or for simple joy. The joy of risks, the more personal the better, was never far from him, any more than the excitement of ideas. The most important step in his life was a signal instance of this, as we may discern in the light of *The Amateur Emigrant* and *Across the Plains*, the picture of the conditions in which he fared from England to California to be married. Here, as always, the great note is the heroic mixture—the thing he *saw*, morally as well as imaginatively; action and performance, at any cost, and the cost made immense by want of health and want of money, illness and anxiety of the extremest kind, and by unsparing sensibilities and perceptions. He had been launched into the world for a fighter with the organism of, say, a 'composer,' though, also, it must be added, with a beautiful saving sanity.

It is doubtless after his settlement in Samoa that his letters have most to give, but there are things they throw off from the first that strike the note above all characteristic, show his imagination always at play, for drollery or philosophy, with his circumstances. The difficulty in writing of him under the personal impression is to suggest enough how directly his being the genius that he was, kept counting in it. In 1879 he writes from Monterey to Mr. Edmund Gosse, in reference to certain grave symptoms of illness:

'I may be wrong, but . . . I believe I must go. . . . But death is no bad friend; a few aches and gasps, and we are done; like the truant child, I am beginning to grow weary and timid in this big, jostling city, and could run to my nurse, even although she should have to whip me before putting me to bed.'

This charming renunciation expresses itself at the very time his talent was growing finer; he was so fond of the sense of youth and the idea of play that he saw whatever happened to him in images and figures, in the terms, almost, of the sports of childhood.

'Are you coming over again to see me some day soon? I keep returning, and now hand over fist, from the realms of Hades. I saw that gentleman between the eyes, and fear him less after each visit. Only Charon and his rough boatmanship I somewhat fear.'

This fear remained with him, sometimes greater, sometimes less, during the first years after his marriage, those spent abroad and in England in health resorts, and it marks constantly, as one may say, one end of the range of his humour—the humour always busy at the other end with the impatience of timidities and precautions, and the vision and invention of essentially open-air situations. It was the possibility of the open-air situation that at last appealed to him as the cast worth staking all for—as to which, as usual, in his admirable rashnesses, he was extraordinarily justified.

'No man but myself knew all my bitterness in those days. Remember that, the next time you think I regret my exile. . . . Remember the pallid brute that lived in Skerryvore like a weevil in a biscuit.'

He found, after a wonderful, adventurous quest, the treasure island, the climatic paradise that met, that enhanced, his possibilities; and with this discovery was ushered in his completely full and rich period, the time in which—as the wondrous whimsicality and spontaneity of his correspondence testify—his genius and his character most overflowed. He had done as well for himself in his appropriation of Samoa as if he had done it for the hero of a novel, only with the complications and braveries actual and palpable. 'I have no more hope in anything'—and this in the midst of magnificent production—'than a dead frog; I go into everything with a composed despair, and don't mind—just as I always go to sea with the conviction I am to be drowned, and like it before all other pleasures.' He could go to sea as often as he liked and not be spared such hours as one of these pages vividly evokes—those of the joy of fictitious composition in an otherwise prostrating storm, amid the crash of the elements and with his grasp of his subject, but too needfully sacrificed, it might have appeared, to his clutch of seat and inkstand.

'If only I could secure a violent death, what a fine success! I wish to die in my boots; no more Land of Counterpane for me. To be drowned, to be shot, to be thrown from a horse—aye, to be hanged, rather than pass again through that slow dissolution.'

He speaks in one of the *Vailima Letters*, Mr. Colvin's publication of 1895, to which it is one of the offices of these volumes promptly to make us return, of one of his fictions as a 'long, tough yarn with some pictures of the manners of to-day in the greater world—not the shoddy, sham world of cities, clubs and colleges, but the world where men still live a man's life.' That is distinct, and in the same letter he throws off a summary of all that, in his final phase, satisfied and bribed him, which is as significant as it is racy. His correspondent, as was inevitable now and then for his friends at home, appears to have indulged in one of those harmless pointings of the moral—as to the distant dangers he *would* court—by which we all were more or less moved to relieve ourselves of the depressed consciousness that he could do beautifully without us, and that our collective tameness was far (which indeed was distinctly the case) from forming his proper element. There is no romantic life for which something amiable has not to be sweepingly sacrificed, and of *us*, in our inevitable category, the sweep, practically, was clean.

'Your letter had the most wonderful "I told you so" I ever heard in the course of my life. Why, you madman, I wouldn't change my present installation for any post, dignity, honour, or advantage conceivable to me. It fills the bill; I have the loveliest time. And as for wars and rumours of wars, you surely know enough of me to be aware that I like that also a thousand times better than decrepit peace in Middlesex. I do not quite like politics. I am too aristocratic, I fear, for that. God knows I don't care who I chum with; perhaps like sailors best; but to go round and sue and sneak to keep a crowd together—never.'

His categories satisfied him; he had got hold of 'the world where men still live a man's life'—which was not, as we have just seen, that of 'cities, clubs and colleges.' He was supremely suited, in short, at last—at the cost, of course, of simplifications of view that, intellectually, he failed quite exactly (it was one of his few limitations) to measure; but in a way that ministered to his rare capacity for growth, and placed in supreme relief his affinity with the universal romantic. It was not that anything could ever be, for him, plain sailing, but that, at forty, he had been able to turn his life into the fairy tale of achieving, in a climate that he somewhere describes as 'an expurgated heaven,' such a happy physical consciousness as he had never known. This enlarged, in every way, his career, opening the door still wider to that real puss-in-the-corner game of opposites by which we have, critically, the interest of seeing him perpetually agitated. Let me repeat that these new volumes, from the date of his definite expatriation, direct us, for the details of the picture, constantly to the *Vailima Letters*; with as constant an effect of our thanking our fortune—to say nothing of his own —that he should have had in these years a correspondent and a confidant who so beautifully drew him out. If he possessed in Mr. Sidney Colvin his literary *chargé d'affaires* at home, the ideal friend and *alter ego* on whom he could unlimitedly rest, this is a proof the more—with the general rarity of such cases—of what it was in his nature to make people wish to do for him. To Mr. Colvin he is more familiar than to any one, more whimsical and natural and, frequently, more inimitable—of all of which a just notion can be given only by abundant citation. And yet citation itself is embarrassed, with nothing to guide it but his perpetual spirits, perpetual acuteness and felicity, play of fancy and of wisdom. These things make him jump from pole to pole and fairly hum, at times, among the objects and subjects that filled his air, as a charged bee among flowers.

He is never more delightful than when he is most egotistic, most consciously charmed with something he has done.

'And the papers are some of them up to dick, and no mistake. I agree with you, the lights seem a little turned down.'

When we learn that the articles alluded to are those collected in *Across the Plains*, we quite assent to this impression made by them after a troubled interval, and envy the author who, in a far Pacific isle, could see *The Lantern-Bearers*, *A Letter to a Young Gentleman* and *Pulvis et Umbra* float back to him as a guarantee of his faculty and between covers constituting the book that is really to live. Stevenson's masculine wisdom, moreover, his remarkable final sanity, is always—and it was not what made least in him for happy intercourse—close to his comedy and next door to his slang.

'And however low the lights are, the stuff is true, and I

believe the more effective; after all, what I wish to fight is the best fought by a rather cheerless presentation of the truth. The world must return some day to the word "duty," and be done with the word "reward." There are no rewards, and plenty duties. And the sooner a man sees that and acts upon it, like a gentleman or a fine old barbarian, the better for himself.'

It would, perhaps, be difficult to quote a single paragraph giving more than this of the whole of him. But there is abundance of him in this too:

'How do journalists fetch up their drivel? . . . It has taken me two months to write 45,500 words; and, be damned to my wicked prowess, I am proud of the exploit! . . . A respectable little five-bob volume, to bloom unread in shop windows. After that I'll have a spank at fiction. And rest? I shall rest in the grave, or when I come to Italy. If only the public will continue to support me! I lost my chance not dying; there seems blooming little fear of it now. I worked close on five hours this morning; the day before, close on nine; and unless I finish myself off with this letter I'll have another hour and a half, or *aiblins twa*, before dinner. Poor man, how you must envy me as you hear of these orgies of work, and you scarce able for a letter. But Lord! Colvin, how lucky the situations are not reversed, for I have no situation, nor am fit for any. Life is a steigh brae. Here, have at Knappe, and no more clavers!'

If he talked profusely—and this is perfect talk—if he loved to talk, above all, of his work in hand, it was because, though perpetually frail, he was never inert, and did a thing, if he did it at all, with passion. He was not fit, he says, for a situation, but a situation overtook him inexorably at Vailima, and doubtless at last, indeed, swallowed him up. His position, with differences, comparing, in some respects, smaller things to greater, and with fewer differences, after all, than likenesses, his position resembles that of Scott at Abbotsford, just as, sound, sensible and strong, on each side, in spite of the immense gift of dramatic and poetic vision, the earlier and the later man had something of a common nature. Life became bigger, for each, than the answering effort could meet, and in their death they were not divided. Stevenson's late emancipation was, after all, a fairy tale only because he himself was, in his manner, a magician. He liked to touch many matters and to shrink from none; nothing can exceed the impression we get of the things that, in these years, he dealt with, from day to day, as they came up, and the things that, as well, almost without order or relief, he planned and invented, took up and talked of and dropped, took up and talked of and carried through. Had I space to treat myself to a clue for selection from the whole record, there is nothing I should better like it to be than a tracking of his 'literary opinions' and literary projects, the scattered swarm of his views, sympathies, antipathies, *obiter dicta*, as an artist—his flurries and fancies, imaginations, evocations, quick infatuations, as a teller of possible tales. Here is a whole little circle of discussion; but this is a circle in which to engage one's self at all is to be too much engulfed.

His overflow on such matters is, meanwhile, amusing enough as mere spirits and sport—interesting as it would yet be to catch as we might, at different moments, the congruity between the manner of his feeling a fable in the germ and that of his afterward handling it. There are passages, again and again, that light, strikingly, what I should call his general conscious method in his relation, were I not more tempted to call it his conscious—for that is what it seems to come to—want of method. A whole delightful letter (to Mr. Colvin, February 1, 1892) is a vivid type. (This letter, I may mention, is independently notable for the drollery of its allusion to a sense of scandal—of all things in the world—excited in some editorial breast by *The Beach of Falesá*; which leads him to the eminently pertinent remark that 'this is a poison bad world for the romancer, this Anglo-Saxon world; I usually get out of it by not having any women in it at all.' Then he remembers he had *The Treasure of Franchard* refused as unfit for a family magazine and feels —as well he may—'despair weigh upon his wrists.' The despair haunts him and comes out on another occasion. 'Five more chapters of *David*. . . . All love affair; seems pretty good to me. Will it do for the young person? I don't know: since *The Beach*, I know nothing except that men are fools and hypocrites, and I know less of them than I was fond enough to fancy.') A part of his physiognomy, always, is the particularly salient play of his shades of feeling, the way his spirits are set off by his melancholy, and his brave conclusions by his rueful doubts.

He communicates, to his confidant, with the eagerness of a boy, in holidays, confabulating over a Christmas charade; but I remember no instance of his expressing a subject, as one may say, *as* a subject—hinting at what novelists mainly know, I imagine, as the determinant thing in it, the idea out of which it springs. The form, the envelope, is there with him, headforemost, *as* the idea; titles, names, that is, chapters, sequences, orders, while we are still asking ourselves how it was that he primarily put to his own mind what it was all to be about. He simply *felt* this, evidently, and it is always the one dumb sound, the only inarticulate thing, in all his contagious candour. He finds, none the less, in the letter to which I refer, one of the problems of the wonderful projected *Sophia Scarlet* 'exactly a Balzac one, and I wish I had his fist—for I have already a better method—the kinetic—whereas he continually allowed himself to be led into the static.' There we have him—Stevenson, not Balzac—at his most overflowing; and, after all, radiantly capable of conceiving at another moment that his 'better method' would have been none at all for Balzac's vision of a subject—least of all, of *the* subject, the whole of life. Balzac's method was adapted to his notion of presentation—which we may accept, it strikes me, under the protection of what he presents. Were it not, in fine, as I may repeat, to embark in a bigger boat than would here turn round, I might note further that Stevenson has elsewhere—was disposed in general to have—too short a way with this master. There is an interesting passage in which he charges him with having never known what to leave out, a passage which has its bearing on condition of being read with due remembrance of the class of performance to which *Le Colonel Chabert*, for instance, *Le Curé de Tours*, *L'Interdiction*, *La Messe de l'Athée* (to name but a few brief masterpieces) belong.

These, however, are comparatively small questions; *the* impression, for the reader of the later letters, is simply one of singular beauty—of deepening talent, of happier and richer expression, and, above all, of a sort of ironic, desperate gallantry, burning away, with a finer and finer fire, in a strange, alien air and only the more touching to us from his own resolute consumption, as it were, of the smoke. He had incurred great charges, he sailed a ship loaded to the brim, so that the strain under which he lived and wrought was immense; but the very grimness of it all is sunny, slangy, funny, familiar; there is as little of the effusive in his twinges of melancholy as of the priggish in his moments of moralizing. His wisdom on matters of art had sometimes, I think, its lapses, but on matters of life was really winged and inspired. He has a soundness, in this quarter, a soundness all liberal and easy and born of the manly experience, that it is a luxury to touch. There are no compunctions, nor real impatiences, for he had, in a singular degree, got what he wanted, the life absolutely discockneyfied, the situation as romantically 'swagger' as if it had been an imagination made real; but his practical anxieties necessarily spin themselves finer, and it is just this production of the thing imagined that has more and more to meet them. It all hung, the situation, by *that* beautiful, golden thread, the swinging of which in the wind, as he spins it in alternate doubt and elation, we watch with much of the suspense and pity with which we sit at the serious drama. It is serious in the extreme; yet the forcing of production, in the case of a faculty so beautiful and delicate, affects us almost as the straining of a nerve or the distortion of a limb.

'I sometimes sit and yearn for anything in the nature of an income that would come in—mine has all got to be gone and fished for with the immortal mind of man. What I want is the income that really comes in of itself, while all you have to do is just to blossom and exist and sit on chairs. . . . I should probably amuse myself with works that would make your hair curl, if you had any left.'

To read over some of his happiest things, to renew one's sense of the extraordinarily fine temper of his imagination, is to say to one's self, 'What a horse to have to ride every week to market!' We must all go to market, but the most fortunate of us, surely, are those who may drive thither, and on days not too frequent, nor by a road too rough, a ruder and homelier animal. He touches in more than one place—and with notable beauty and real authority in that little mine of felicities, the *Letter to a Young Gentleman*—on the conscience for 'frugality' which should be the artist's finest point of honour; so that one of his complications here was, doubtless, the sense that, on this score, his position had inevitably become somewhat false. The literary romantic is by no means necessarily expensive; but of the many ways in which the practical, the active, has to be paid for, this departure from frugality would be, it is easy to conceive, not the least. And we perceive his recognizing this as he recognized everything—if not in time, then out of it; accepting inconsistency, as he always did, with the gaiety of a man of courage—not being, that is, however intelligent, priggish for logic and the grocer's book any more than for anything else. Only everything made for keeping it up; and it was a great deal to keep up; though when he throws off *The Ebb-Tide* and rises to *Catriona*, and then again to *Weir of Hermiston*, as if he could rise to almost anything, we breathe anew and look longingly forward. The latest of these letters contain such admirable things, testify so to the reach of his intelligence and vibrate so, in short, with genius and charm, that we feel him at moments not only unexhausted but replenished, and capable, perhaps, for all we know to the contrary, of new experiments and deeper notes. The intelligence is so great that he loses nothing; not a gossamer thread of the 'thought of the time' that, wafted to him on the other side of the globe, may not be caught in a branch and played with; he puts such a soul into nature and such human meanings, for comedy and tragedy, into what surrounds him, however shabby or short, that he really lives in society by living in his own perceptions and generosities, or, as we say nowadays, his own atmosphere. In this atmosphere—which seems to have had the gift of abounding the more it was breathed by others—these pages somehow prompt us to see almost every object on his tropic isle bathed and refreshed.

So far, at any rate, from growing thin for want of London, he can transmit to London, or to its neighbourhood, communications such as it would scarce know otherwise where to seek. A letter to his cousin, Mr. R. A. M. Stevenson, of September, 1894, touches so on all things, and, as he would himself have said, so adorns them, brimming over with its happy extravagance of thought, that, far from our feeling Vailima, in the light of it, to be out of the world, it strikes us that the world has moved for the time to Vailima. There is world enough everywhere, he quite unconsciously shows, for the individual, the right one, to be what we call a man of it. He has, like every one not convenienced with the pleasant back-door of stupidity, to make his account with seeing and facing more things, seeing and facing everything, with the unrest of new impressions and ideas, the loss of the fond complacencies of youth.

'But as I go on in life, day by day, I become more of

a bewildered child; I cannot get used to this world, to procreation, to heredity, to sight, to hearing; the commonest things are a burthen. The prim obliterated polite face of life, and the broad, bawdy, and orgiastic—or mænadic—foundations, form a spectacle to which no habit reconciles me; and "I could wish my days to be bound each to each" by the same open-mouthed wonder. They *are* anyway, and whether I wish it or not. . . . I remember very well your attitude to life, this conventional surface of it. You have none of that curiosity for the social stage directions, the trivial *ficelles* of the business; it is simian, but that is how the wild youth of man is captured.'

The whole letter is enchanting.

'But no doubt there is something great in the half-success that has attended the effort of turning into an emotional religion, Bald Conduct, without any appeal, or almost none, to the figurative, mysterious, and constitutive facts of life. Not that conduct is not constitutive, but dear! it's dreary! On the whole, conduct is better dealt with on the cast-iron "gentleman" and duty formula, with as little fervour and poetry as possible; stoical and short.'

The last letter of all, it will have been abundantly noted, has, with one of those characteristically thrown-out references to himself that were always half a whim, half a truth, and all a picture, a remarkable premonition. It is addressed to Mr. Edmund Gosse:

'It is all very well to talk of renunciation, and of course it has to be done. But, for my part, give me a roaring toothache! I do like to be deceived and to dream, but I have very little use for either watching or meditation. I was not born for age.... I am a childless, rather bitter, very clear-eyed, blighted youth. I have, in fact, lost the path that makes it easy and natural for you to descend the hill. I am going at it straight. And where I have to go down it is a precipice.... You can never write another dedication that can give the same pleasure to the vanished Tusitala.'

Two days later he met his end in the happiest form, by the straight, swift bolt of the gods. It was, as all his readers know, with an admirable, unfinished thing in hand, scarce a quarter written—a composition as to which his hopes were, presumably with much justice and as they were by no means always, of the highest. Nothing is more interesting than the rich way in which, in *Weir of Hermiston* and *Catriona*, the predominant imaginative Scot reasserts himself after gaps and lapses, distractions and deflections superficially extreme. There are few backward jumps, in this order, surely, more joyous and *à pieds joints*, or of a kind more interesting to a critic. The imaginative vision is hungry and tender just in proportion as the actual is otherwise beset; so that we must sigh always in vain for the quality that this purified flame, as we call it, would have been able to give the metal. And how many things, to the critic, the case suggests—how many possible reflections cluster about it and seem to take light from it! It was 'romance' indeed, *Weir of Hermiston*, we feel, as we see it only grow in assurance and ease as the reach to it, across all the spaces, becomes more positively artificial. The case is *literary*, with intensity, and, given the nature of the talent, only thereby the more beautiful: he embroiders in silk and silver—in defiance of climate and nature, of near every aspect, and with such another antique needle as was nowhere, least of all in those latitudes, to be bought—in the intervals of wondrous international and insular politics and of fifty material cares and complications. His special stock of association, most personal style and most unteachable trick fly away again to him like so many strayed birds to nest, each with the flutter, in its beak, of some scrap of document or legend, some fragment of picture or story, to be retouched, revarnished and reframed.

These things he does with a gusto, moreover, for which, after all, his literary treatment of the islands and the island life had ever vainly waited. Curious enough that his years of the tropics and his fraternity with the natives never drew from him any such 'rendered' view as might have been looked for in advance. For the absent and vanished Scotland he *has* the image—within the limits (too narrow ones, we may perhaps judge) admitted by his particular poetic; but the law of these things, in him, was, as of many others, amusingly, conscientiously perverse. The Pacific, in which he materially delighted, made him, 'descriptively,' serious and even rather dry; with his own country, on the other hand, materially impossible, he was ready infinitely to play. He easily sends us back again here to our vision of his mixture. There was only one thing on earth that he loved as much as literature—which was the total absence of it; and to the present, the immediate, whatever it was, he always made the latter offering. Samoa was susceptible of no 'style'—none of that, above all, with which he was most conscious of an affinity—save the demonstration of its rightness for life; and this left the field abundantly clear for the Border, the Great North Road and the eighteenth century. I have been reading over *Catriona* and *Weir* with the purest pleasure with which we can follow a man of genius—that of seeing him abound in his own sense. In *Weir* especially, like an improvising pianist, he superabounds and revels, and his own sense, by a happy stroke, appeared likely never more fully and brightly to justify him; to have become even in some degree a new sense, with new chords and possibilities. It is the 'old game,' but it is the old game that he exquisitely understands. The figure of Hermiston is creative work of the highest order, those of the two Kirsties, especially that of the elder, scarce less so; and we ache for the loss of a thing which could give out such touches as the quick joy, at finding herself in falsehood, of the enamoured girl whose brooding elder brother has told her that as soon as she has a lover she will begin to lie (' "Will I have gotten my jo now?" she thought with secret rapture'); or a passage so richly charged with imagination as that in which the young lover recalls her as he has first seen and desired her, seated at grey of evening on an old tomb in the moorland, and unconsciously making him think, by her scrap of song, both of his mother, who sang it and whom he has lost, and

'of their common ancestors now dead, of their rude wars composed, their weapons buried with them, and of these strange changelings, their descendants, who lingered a little in their places and would soon be gone also, and perhaps sung of by others at the gloaming hour. By one of the unconscious arts of tenderness the two women were enshrined together in his memory. Tears, in that hour of sensibility, came into his eyes indifferently at the thought of either; and the girl, from being something merely bright and shapely, was caught up into the zone of things serious as life and death and his dead mother. So that, in all ways and on either side, Fate played his game artfully with this poor pair of children. The generations were prepared, the pangs were made ready, before the curtain rose on the dark drama.'

It is not a tribute that Stevenson would have appreciated, but I may not forbear noting how closely such a page recalls many another in the tenderest manner of Pierre Loti. There would not, compared, be a pin to choose between them. How, we at all events ask ourselves as we consider *Weir*, could he have kept it up?—while the reason for which he didn't, reads itself back into his text as a kind of beautiful, rash divination in him that he needn't. Among prose fragments it stands quite alone, with the particular grace and sanctity of mutilation worn by the marble morsels of masterwork in another art. This and the other things, of his best, he left; but these things, lovely as, on rereading many of them at the suggestion of his Correspondence, they are, are not the whole, or more than the half, of his abiding charm. The finest papers in *Across the Plains*, in *Memories and Portraits*, in *Virginibus Puerisque*, stout of substance and supremely silver of speech, have both a nobleness and a nearness that place them, for perfection and roundness, above his fictions, and that also may well remind a vulgarized generation of what, even under its nose, English prose can be. But it is bound up with his name, for our wonder and reflection, that he is something other than the author of this or that particular beautiful thing, or of all such things together. It has been his fortune (whether or no the greatest that can befall a man of letters) to have had to consent to become, by a process not purely mystic and not wholly untraceable—what shall we call it?—a Figure. Tracing is needless now, for the personality has acted and the incarnation is full. There he is—he has passed ineffaceably into happy legend. This case of the figure is of the rarest, and the honour surely of the greatest. In all our literature we can count them, sometimes with the work and sometimes without. The work has often been great and yet the figure *nil*. Johnson was one, and Goldsmith and Byron; and the two former, moreover, not in any degree, like Stevenson, in virtue of

the element of grace. Was it this element that settled the business even for Byron? It seems doubtful; and the list, at all events, as we approach our own day, shortens and stops. Stevenson has it at present—may we not say?—
—pretty well to himself, and it is not one of the scrolls in which he least will live.

See Alphonse Dudet NOTES ON LIFE(tr'd 1900)

See Alphonse Daudet:NOTES ON LIFE(tr'd 1900)on the visit to London in May 1895 after the paralysis had already caused gt suffering.He describe the visit to Windsor,to AC Benson(unhappily out) to Box Hill to see Meredith who hummed as he walk needed support,so that to Daudet,this novelist & himself both trailed the wing like wounded gulls: and cd scarcely be spoken with bec the drawbridge of his deafness was always up."He speaks more slowly in French with mouth wider open,as if our words were of smaller dimensions than those of th English.Never to be forgotten,that visit to Box Hill
On the way back(IBID 411) !! J tells about the life of Stevenson at Samoa: a return to primitive existence,his wife & her mother living in gandour as, a sort of night-dress,hair loose over the showers. A yg midshipman to whom Stevenson hd given letter of introduction to HJ—arrived at his hous or 5 mos after Stevenson's death. " So" said the graceful writer[412]"one Sunday morning I had at breakfast a fine,bronzed yg fellow,who brot me th latest new of the dear friend already wept for ma a day.